FIGHT THE BEAST

The Proven System for Quitting Porn and Other Sexual Addictions

Heather Nielsen

ISBN: 9798813946714

Printed in the U.S.A.

No part of this publication may be reproduced or distributed in any form or by any means, or stored in a database or retrieval system, without the prior written permission of the publisher. Exceptions are made for brief excerpts used in published reviews.

This book is designed to provide accurate and authoritative information with regard to the subject matter covered. It is sold with the understanding that the publisher and/or author are not engaged in rendering medical or professional advice.

Neither Heather Nielsen nor Fight The Beast can be held responsible for loss or injury as a result of any unsafe behavior by any reader who undertakes to recreate any action described in this publication. Using the information contained within the text of this book is done solely at the reader's own risk.

Registered trademarks and trademarks are the property of the registered trademark and trademark owners.

© 2022 Heather Nielsen, Fight The Beast

Let Us Support You!

Please accept our invitation to benefit from the supportive community at **FightTheBeast.org**

Decades of research have proven that recovery from addiction is easier and happens faster when you are surrounded by a positive support network of like-minded people.

Visit: www.FightTheBeast.org

The author is available for a limited number of educational and inspirational **speaking engagements** about addiction and recovery from pornography.

For more information, visit: **www.FightTheBeast.org/speaking**

Acknowledgements

My heartfelt thanks and appreciation go to the following who made this book possible:

First, to my kids W., A., and S., for all they've sacrificed in support of *Fight The Beast*.

Second, to the many donors of time, funds, and encouragement, that have helped along the way.

TABLE OF CONTENTS

Introduction 1

Section 1: Planning for Your 30-Day Journey

    Why "30 Days"? 16
    How To Navigate This Book: 17
    Key Definitions 18
    Key Principles 19
    Preparing to Quit...28
    Game Plan..30
    Coping With Urges 31
    Rewiring Your Brain...39
    Your Relationship With God 44
    Frequently Asked Questions..46
    Final Miscellaneous Tips 49
    Time to Commit! 50
    My Game Plan...52

Section 2: Overcoming Relapse

    This Is A Shame Free Zone. Period. 56
    Bouncing Back from Relapse 59
    Relapse Is for Learning 60

Section 3: Your First 7 Days

    Day 1 - One Step At A Time..68
    Day 2 - The Biggest Mistake You Can Make...................71
    Day 3 - Visualization 74
    Day 4 - Figuring Out Your Deeper Needs......................78
    Day 5 - One MORE Day at a Time 84
    Day 6 - Recurring Negative Thoughts...........................86
    Day 7 - Using Your Sexual Energy for Success..............92
    Day 8 - Time to Celebrate!..95

Section 4: Reaching 30 Days & Beyond

- 9. Keeping Sexuality in Proper Perspective 99
- 10. Life IS a Challenge 103
- 11. The Dangers of Lust 108
- 12. Real Love 112
- 13. Beasts & Dragons: There is No Immunity 116
- 14. Forgiveness 118
- Day 15. Review Your Progress, Reason, & Plan 122
- 16. Balancing The Past, Present, and Future 128
- 17. Defining Yourself: Who are you? 141
- 18. Ego: The Enemy Within 144
- 19. Confidence & Attractiveness 150
- 20. Humility & Modesty 157
- 21. Leaving Your Comfort Zone 160
- 22. Loneliness 161
- 23. Discovering Your Values 165
- 24. What Sex Is, Isn't & Should Be 173
- 25. Making Amends 177
- 26. The Purpose of Doubt 180
- 27. Habits & Muscle Memory 184
- 28. Gratitude 185
- 29. Natural Law 188
- 30. Pride vs. Healthy Self-Esteem 191
- Day 30 Clean: Do you want to continue? 195

Additional Daily Review Pages

INTRODUCTION

Imagine for a moment you're taken hostage at gunpoint. Your captors bring you to an interrogation style room, containing nothing but a table, chair, and a laptop connected to the Internet. One of the captors waves a gun in the air and pulls the trigger. Bam! The noise is deafening. You're terrified of what they're going to do next.

Then comes another shock.

Your captors proceed to tell you that your entire family is hostage in the next room, and you're given a simple instruction: *"You may use the laptop, and browse any websites you wish, but know that we'll be monitoring you remotely. The moment you choose to search for and look at porn OR touch yourself, we'll kill your entire family."*

Okay, aside from being a strange set of kidnappers, humor me for a moment and consider the scenario.

What would you do, knowing you struggle with porn? Would you give in, or would you have the self-control to resist?

Even with the extreme stress at that moment, I'm absolutely positive that you'd be able to resist the temptation to look at porn. In fact, knowing what's at stake, there's a high likelihood you may not even use the laptop at all, and if you did, you certainly wouldn't watch anything remotely sexual.

Am I right in that assumption?

Wow! Think about that. We've just proven in less than one minute that *you do possess the self-control and power necessary to stop looking at porn*. So, why has it been so difficult to quit until now? What's different about the hostage situation that made it easy to avoid it?

It's actually very simple... **You had a powerful, motivating reason.**

We'll come back to this scenario soon, but first, I want to say…

Congratulations!

Yes, congratulations. You deserve sincere acknowledgement for taking this important step to improve your life. Although you may be coming from a dark place full of regret, today marks the start of your incredible journey to success and healing. It takes a lot of courage, strength, determination, and humility to make these changes. So, thank you for choosing to make the world a better place, and thank you for being a man or woman of principle and character.

I need to let you know up front that this challenge is not for the faint of heart. It will test you mentally and physically, and may even expose your deepest fears and weaknesses. That's a necessary part of recovery, but don't panic! I'll guide you through the process step-by-step as you unlock your inner potential. The great news is that along the journey, you'll experience incredible benefits such as greater confidence, energy, and creativity. You'll also balance your hormones, lessening anxiety and stress, and ultimately, you'll be able to connect more deeply with both yourself and others. Sounds great, right?!

Fighting addiction is a battle that no one should have to fight alone. Be assured that regardless of how many times you've tried, struggled, and failed in the past, you can and will get through this! This book is your first step in preparing for that war, and at FightTheBeast.org you can find additional tools including coaching, classes, and a wonderful community of love and support. You are the HERO in your *success story*, and now you're also a part of an ever-growing community of like-minded people who are dramatically improving their lives.

I strongly encourage you to visit, explore, and connect with our supportive community network today at **www.FightTheBeast.org**. There are hundreds of thousands of people who understand on a deep level what you're going through, and believe it or not, they are happy to support you!

Why "Fight The Beast"?

Why is this program called "Fight the Beast"? Who or what exactly is the 'beast'?

The *beast* is ultimately the darkness which lies within each of us, causing pain, fear, depression, shame, envy, despondency, hate, and even self-destruction. Your 'beast' might be the compulsive viewing of pornography, masturbation, *or any other addiction, vice, or negative mindset* that's holding you back from achieving your true potential. It is a formidable foe, that at times may even be *indistinguishable* from our own thoughts and desires — an attack from within — making it difficult to understand and overcome.

One dictionary defines the word beast as, *"Something formidably difficult to control or deal with."* (Merriam Webster Dictionary)

Porn and masturbation certainly come under that category, don't they!?

I also want to point out here what the beast is *NOT*. While your personal beast(s) may involve porn or sexual addiction, *the beast **is NOT sexual desire or affection***. This is an important distinction to understand, here's why.

Many in recovery become frustrated when the urge to relapse returns. These urges and thoughts, however, **do not make you a bad person**. In fact, we all have them. They are an inescapable part of human nature, and they're imprinted in our biology (even certain gut bacteria have been shown to increase sexual urges!)

Sex is an integral and positive part of our identities. It is how we show love, and of course, how children are conceived. It is even *divine*. Saved for the right time and place, sexual relations in a loving and healthy relationship are a powerful and beautiful bonding experience. By contrast, **porn is a toxic poison, a life-sucking leech, and an act of self-harm.**

Therefore, the beast is not *sexuality*, but the desire, or habit of **acting on those impulses** in a way that is **physically, spiritually, or mentally unhealthy and harmful.**

> *"In masturbation there is nothing but loss. There is no reciprocity. There is merely the spending away of a certain force, and no return. The body remains, in a sense, a corpse after the act of self-abuse. There is no change, only deadening."* — D.H. Lawrence, famous writer and poet

Think of it this way: you don't fail a diet by simply being *offered* a restricted food or even wanting it. The harm is done only by *giving in to it.* So, this book is designed to help you **develop better habits, guard against temptation, reduce unwanted urges, and build a healthier, happier life!**

How Big is The Problem of Pornography?

It's truly shocking how pervasive and permeating pornography addiction has become, largely due to the Internet and the scale of its use now is jaw-dropping. Consider these figures:

- In the United States alone, two hard-core pornographic movies are released *every hour.*
- 25% of all online searches and 35% of all downloads are related to pornography.
- According to the National Coalition for the Protection of Children & Families, 2010, 47% of families in the United States reported that pornography is a problem in their home.
- 68% of divorce cases involve one party meeting someone over the Internet, while 56% involve one party having an "obsessive interest" in porn.
- The average child is now first exposed to Internet porn at age 11.
- Under the age of 10 accounts for 22% of the porn consumption of minors

The rapid growth of the porn industry, now reaching younger audiences more than ever, has contributed to the dramatic increase in sexual addictions, gender dysmorphia, sexual orientation crisis, and broken families. Communities and workplaces are also struggling with the proliferation of sexual harassment cases, which are proven to be influenced by porn consumption.

Where Does Porn Addiction Start?

For many, their first exposure to porn happens in their early teens, sometimes even earlier. Jordan was only 11 years old when a friend first introduced him to porn. Although he felt bad about it, something about the experience was exciting and intriguing. As he went through puberty, the increased sexual hormones led him to crave it more and more until masturbation became a regular habit.

In college, he began using it to cope with stress and loneliness — sometimes even multiple times a day. He thought that his only real *problem* was not having a sexually active relationship; however, his addiction persisted even after marriage.

While married, he often felt guilty, ashamed, and dishonest about his addiction which he hid from his wife. This led to increased frustration, frequent fights over nothing, trust issues, and ultimately divorce.

Unfortunately, his story is not unique. It is shared by millions of men and women also struggling to quit pornography. The good news is, though, that his story didn't end there! After hitting rock bottom, Jordan became keenly interested in recovery, joined *Fight The Beast*, and committed to taking recovery seriously. He wanted to become a new man and start a new life without addiction or pornography.

Recovery was difficult at first, however after reaching 30 days, he became far more confident and disciplined. The benefits he gained far outweighed any temptation he had to use porn, and he went on to achieve a more permanent state of recovery.

Can you relate to Jordan's story and struggles with porn? If so, we'll next look at establishing your own reasons for quitting.

Why Quit?

There are *many* critical reasons to quit looking at porn. For starters, porn kills love, and really a lot of other things too. It's mentally, emotionally, spiritually, and even physically numbing. Long-term, it destroys relationships and marriages.

Patrick Fagan, a psychologist who has spent more than a decade researching the effects of porn, says: *"Pornography hurts adults, children, couples, families, and society. Among adolescents, pornography hinders the development of a healthy sexuality, and among adults, it distorts sexual attitudes and social realities. In families, pornography use leads to marital dissatisfaction, infidelity, separation, and divorce."*

Although we won't get into the brain science in this book, you might also do research on the medical terms: hyperfrontation, adrenal fatigue, habituation, desensitization, porn addiction's effect on the brain, and porn induced erectile dysfunction. Many of these areas are still undergoing research, while others have already shown serious negative effects of porn use.

But rather than dwell on the negative aspects which you are no doubt aware of, let's focus on the positive effects of quitting. Rather than sharing my own beliefs, it may be helpful for you to hear directly from some of my students. Thousands of people have transformed their lives with recovery, and here's a snapshot of their experiences, in their own words:

"My focus has improved significantly."

"My productivity has improved dramatically."

"My mental health is so much better, and I no longer feel depressed."

"My self-control has improved significantly, and I now make better choices."

"My values have changed in a good way. If something isn't right, I take the time to make it right."

"I feel a lot more clarity and less distraction."

"I'm making better eye contact with people, and I feel more confident in social situations."

"I feel better about myself."

"*My exercise workouts have improved.*"

"*I have lost so much weight that everyone keeps asking me, 'What diet are you on?' The truth? The porn diet. It's changed everything!*"

"*I went from seeing nobody and being really depressed about a lack of intimacy, to having an extremely promising relationship.*"

"*I feel like a better parent. I am able to bond with my daughter much better than before.*"

"*I can deal with challenges more effectively.*"

"*I respect people more in general, but I especially appreciate the beauty in the opposite sex.*"

"*I don't feel the need to rush. I enjoy taking the time to develop a conversation, and I enjoy socializing more than I have in a long time.*"

This is an incredible array of positive comments about the benefits from quitting porn, and these are just a few of the benefits YOU can look forward to as you begin recovery.

Learning From "Hall of Fame" Men

When I first got involved with the porn-recovery and semen retention community, I came across a comment that completely changed the way I viewed abstinence.

One Reddit, user r/Malesromm asked the question: *"Could you imagine great men like Socrates, Abraham Lincoln, or MLK sitting behind a computer monitor for three hours straight, watching porn, and fapping?"*

Well, these great men *didn't*. In fact, many, if not most, of the world's "Hall of Fame" men have practiced semen retention or sexual abstinence at one point or another! Many even attributed their **success** to sexual discipline, citing that it gave them the time, energy, creativity, and other resources to change the world and achieve greatness. Learning this caused a dramatic shift in the way I viewed sexual abstinence. I realized that quitting porn is not a shameful journey of "recovery," but a powerful **tool for success!**

Here are a few inspiring quotes from some of these "Hall of Fame" men against porn and masturbation:

David Haye, Heavyweight Boxer — "I don't ejaculate for six weeks before the fight. No sex, no masturbation, no nothing. It releases too much tension. It releases a lot of minerals and nutrients that your body needs, and it releases them cheaply. Releasing weakens the knees and your legs. Find a lion that hasn't had some food for a while, and you've got a dangerous cat. So, there won't be a drip from me. Even in my sleep — if there are girls all over me in my dream, I say to them, 'I've got a fight next week, I can't do anything. I can't do it.' That's control. I've been doing that since I was fifteen and its part and parcel of my preparation now. That's why I am who I am today — it's down to all those little sacrifices. Find me another boxer who makes that sacrifice, and you'll find another champion."

Georg Hackenschmidt, 20th Century Strongman, Wrestler and Philosopher — "Moderation in sexual intercourse is very important. Sexual abstemiousness should be strictly observed during the early age of manhood and development. He who observes this recommendation will soon benefit by the immense prerogatives of chastity. A few years ago, a colleague of mine said to me: "Nonsense, that is only human nature." This "clever" man, however, reached only a secondary position as a strong man, and now, at the age of thirty, he is actually degenerating as an athlete."

Henry David Thoreau, Poet and Philosopher — "The generative energy, which, when we are loose, dissipates and makes us unclean, when we are continent invigorates and inspires us. Chastity is the flowering of man; and what are called Genius, Heroism, Holiness, and the like, are but various fruits which succeed it."

Isaac Newton, Mathematician, Physicist, Astronomer, and Author — In a letter to John Locke, Newton wrote, "The way to chastity is not to struggle with incontinent thoughts but to avert the thoughts by some employment, or by reading, or by meditating on other things."

Jesus Christ, Christian Leader — "But I say to you that everyone who keeps looking at a woman so as to have a passion for her, has already committed adultery with her in his heart."

Jean-Jacques Rousseau, Philosopher, Writer, Composer — "If once he acquires this dangerous supplement (masturbation addiction), he is lost. From then on, body and soul will be enervated; he will carry to the grave the sad effects of this habit, the most fatal habit which a young man can be subjected to."

Immanuel Kant, German Philosopher in the Age of Enlightenment — "The ground of proving is to be sought, no doubt, in this, that man meanly abdicates his personality, when he attempts to employ himself as a bare means to satisfy a brutal lust."

"[He] resigns himself an abandoned outcast to brutality, enjoying his own self-abuse — that is, he makes himself an object of abomination, and stands bereft of all reverence of any kind."

Leonardo Da Vinci, Painter — "You will never have a greater or lesser dominion than that over yourself... the height of a man's success is gauged by his self-mastery; the depth of his failure by his self-abandonment. ...And this law is the expression of eternal justice. He who cannot establish dominion over himself will have no dominion over others."

Mark Twain, Author — "If you must gamble your lives sexually, don't play a lone hand too much. When you feel a revolutionary uprising in your system, get your Vendome Column down some other way — don't jerk it down."

Mark Wahlberg, Actor and Singer — "I don't get down with jerking off, dude. I lead a clean and pure life.... Look, I don't believe in everything that the church says. I try to do the right thing. I lead a clean and pure life. I'm a married guy. I have a beautiful wife. Sex is not the most important thing to me..."

Mike Tyson, Fighter — "I never knew that conquering so many women takes so much from you more than adds so much to you. I always read that the great fighters never had sex before fights and I was a young kid and I wanted to be the youngest heavyweight champion in the world, so I restrained myself from sex for around five years."

Saigō Takamori, Samurai and Nobleman — (Talking about himself) "He saw abstinence as empowering rather than constraining...In his youth Saigo saw sex not as pleasurable dissipation or intimacy but as an impediment to happiness and loyalty."

Swami Vivekananda, Hindu Monk — "You may wonder what made them do this, you may wonder if I had some strange power. Let me tell you that I did have a power and this is it — never once in my life did I allow myself to have even one sexual thought. I trained my mind, my thinking, and the powers that man usually uses along that line I put into a higher channel, and it developed a force so strong that nothing could resist it

Winston Churchill, Christian Author — "The reason that I can write so much is that I don't waste my essence in the bedroom."

50 Cent, Rapper — "Step 1. To avoid the urge to masturbate, stop going to porn sites. Step 2. Make a conscious decision not to turn your head after people walk by you. Step 3. Do not go to strip clubs. Step 4. Do not look at lust filled magazines."

While these men were not perfect, and you may disagree with their individual philosophies and choices, their influence and success are undisputed. These men have all had an impact on the world and found success in their own fields, but they all started with ***conquering themselves first.***

Choosing YOUR Reason

I cannot stress this point enough: Finding your reason (and a GOOD reason) is the single most important part of the quitting process.

It's so critical that I'm going to repeat it for you:

Finding a GOOD reason to quit is the single most important part of the process.

Why is having a reason so important?

In the face of strong urges and temptations, your *reason* for quitting will be your source of strength and influence you to push through. Having a reason that resonates and motivates you will be like a lighthouse through the storms of withdrawals and urges to keep you focused. It is the foundation of the entire process. It is your *reason*.

So, what are some good reasons for quitting?

Would you like to improve your mental or physical health? Would you like to take back control of your schedule, becoming more productive and successful? Do you want to rebalance your hormones to overcome anxiety, depression and stress? Do you desire to improve your connection with your partner? Perhaps if porn has already ruined a past relationship, maybe you want to prevent the same thing happening again? If you're religious, would you like to draw closer to God and feel the peace and happiness of having a clear conscience? Or do you want to shun an industry that is at the center of human trafficking, abuse, and many other serious crimes?

Perhaps more than one of these reasons resonate with you, or perhaps you have a different reason. Whatever the case, take some time to really lock in your reason. **Having a powerful, motivating reason is the #1 key to your success.**

Webster's Dictionary definition for addiction reads: *"To devote; to dedicate. To apply oneself habitually."*

If addiction is a 'practice' you've been devoted to, then in order to quit, you must be *more* dedicated to your reason for quitting. Your compelling reason must become your *new devotion*.

Obviously, what you've just learned requires deep thought in order to make a good decision. Don't rush this process, please take it seriously. Your future happiness and success are at stake.

Stating YOUR Reason(s)

Start by listing the reasons your addiction or habit has negatively impacted yourself and others:

_____

_____

_____

_____

Next, what benefits are you looking forward to as a result of recovery? List all that apply and have meaning for you:

_____

_____

_____

_____

_____

Now, note your main reason(s) for embarking on this journey:

_____

_____

_____

_____

Finally, fill in the blanks:

I want to quit porn (or other sexual addictions) because I acknowledge the negative repercussions, and I strongly believe that _____ is more important to me than relapse.

I commit to being patient, staying focused, and to keep pushing forward. When I do that, I know I will be able to reach my goal and feel/have/be:
_____.

I look forward to reaching 30 days porn free because:

_____

_____

_____

_____

Great job, well done! How do those statements make you feel? Are you excited to start living again!? Do you feel a greater sense of resolve?

I encourage you to write the statements out formally, and put them in a place where you can see them regularly. Repeat them to yourself often. Take them to heart.

If you don't feel moved and motivated by your reason(s), try exploring better reasons. Before you begin the 30-day challenge, you need to have a solid reason to ensure success and a positive experience!

Now, check the relevant box below...

☐ "I feel confident! Let's proceed."

☐ "I'm still unsure and need more time to think/research.

Section 1

Preparing for Your 30-Day Journey

Why "30 Days"?

In this book I often reference quitting for "30 days" and you may be thinking, *"Heather, I am looking to quit porn forever, not just for 30 days."* And I agree! But before you run, you first need to learn to walk. Before quitting forever, comes your first 30 days, which are undoubtedly the hardest. However, after mastering your first 30 days, there's a good chance you'll be able to hit your long-term goals as well!

I encourage you to think of these "30 days" as an experiment. You will encounter many challenges, but you'll also experience incredible benefits. At the end of the 30 days, you will have the opportunity to evaluate how you feel, and decide whether you want to continue the journey to *full recovery*.

Through working with countless people in the process of recovery, I've discovered that there is definitely something significant about the first 30 days. It's only at that benchmark that you'll be able to clearly weigh the pros and cons with full awareness and understanding. Giving up before then will prevent you from being able to *experience* many of the benefits of recovery, so it's vitally important that you do your best to complete the 30-day challenge. Even if you slip up, keep working at it until you succeed with the full 30 days.

In many cases, I recommend focusing on smaller goals and benchmarks along the way such as 4 or 8 days at a time, which we will discuss in more depth soon. However, 30 days is the *minimum abstinence* goal I suggest reaching before deciding if you want to quit.

> **Important note:** As with all other strategies in this book, *if this mindset does not work for you*, feel free to change it for a more **effective** strategy, one that produces better results for *you*. The goal is your recovery, and you have a unique way of thinking and unique needs to consider. Not every strategy works for every person. My recommendation is to have an open mind and *try it out first,* and then if you notice a **negative** effect on your mental health or progress, try a different strategy until you find one that works.

Again, congratulations for taking this important step towards recovery, to become a better you! I'm confident you won't regret it.

HOW TO NAVIGATE THIS BOOK:

Note: This eBook format is not recommend for optimal recovery. That's because recording your answers to journal questions and prompts is a critical part of re-wiring your brain. In order for this book to help you achieve optimal results, you will need an accompanying journal (paper or digital) to record your thoughts on each of the journal activities.

This book is divided into three parts. First, we'll set the scene to understand what's really going on with your addiction, and you'll discover some invaluable tools and strategies that will help you on your path to recovery.

The second part guides you through a 30-day journey. With daily guidance based on our proven system, you'll learn how to stay clean and become purposefully aligned with your mind and body.

Throughout the book you'll find the following five helpful tools as a part of the process of recovery. Even if you don't understand the reason for some of these elements, I urge you to follow the directions and commit to being "all in."

Here's an overview of the **5 tools:**

1. **Journaling:** Self-reflection questions allow you to explore your own thoughts and feelings and assist you on your road to recovery. You can use the writing spaces provided in this book or keep a separate paper or digital journal to record and save your thoughts.

2. **Activities:** Activities and challenges will help you heal, explore your thoughts, and emotions, and rewire your brain. You will want to refer back to some of these activities as you make progress.

3. **Meditation:** In this program, meditation is simply the exploration and discipline of your mind in a way that is constructive and healing. Daily meditation can be a great tool to handle both urges and negative thoughts.

4. **Affirmations:** Affirmations are powerful phrases to say to yourself throughout the day or during a scheduled meditation session. As you do this, you will gradually internalize the key concepts you're learning and build your confidence and peace.

5. **Daily Review:** This section is meant for you to reflect on your progress and record your responses/observations.

KEY DEFINITIONS

Addiction: There is a lot of debate regarding what qualifies as an "addiction" and how the word should be used. For the purposes of this book, and for simplicity's sake, we use the word "addiction" to refer to any habitual or compulsive use of a rewarding stimulus despite recognized adverse consequences. Even if you don't identify with the word "addiction," you may feel free to replace it with the words *habit* or *struggle* as you work through this program.

PMO: This is a commonly used acronym that describes porn, masturbation, and orgasm either together, or individually.

Pornography: Pornography comes in many forms, including books, photos, video, and even audio. For example, many women read erotic fiction while not even realizing it's a form of pornography, and that it can easily lead to addiction.

Sexual addiction: This guide is meant to be used as a resource for all sexual addictions, not just pornography. The terms *pornography* and *sexual addiction* are almost interchangeable throughout this book.

Relapse: What qualifies as a relapse? When should you reset an *abstinence streak*? A relapse occurs anytime you <u>*prematurely break a commitment of abstinence*</u>. If you commit to not watching porn and give in, it's a relapse. However, if you commit to no nudity, and you *accidentally* see something, but look away and/or block the content, it would not be considered a relapse. In another case, you might commit to no masturbation, but begin to touch yourself "a little". In that circumstance, it would only be considered a relapse if you break the initial terms of your own commitment.

KEY PRINCIPLES

The Only Real Addiction

In this book, we're going to break down why you have an addiction or struggle, what to do about it, and how to move forward. The information you'll learn will genuinely change your life, but you must be ready for it.

What if you're not sure you're ready? Let's examine that thought for a moment.

We all face different challenges and addictions, but there is one addiction common to us all: ***our addiction to pain.*** Sounds strange, right? Let me explain...

Be it pride, complacency, laziness, immaturity, fear, weakness, or pain itself, there is something in each of us that sometimes simply does not *want* to move forward and doesn't *want* to grow. It's the reason we sometimes don't listen to others who are genuinely trying to help, and we fail to do things we know we should. It's also the reason we tend to hold onto grief and anger, instead of choosing freedom and happiness. Yes, *pain* is our common addiction.

In moments of brokenness, forgiveness and healing are already there, and yet we often deny ourselves that freedom, choosing pain instead. It's not a conscious choice of course, but it's still a choice happening within our minds. So, how do you overcome the feeling of not *wanting* to change?

Part of the challenge is our instinctive need to defend our self-image and ego. No one wants to be perceived as wrong or weak, so we defend ourselves by denying our flaws and resisting growth. If we're honest, we each know there's a list of things we should work on, but it's easier to procrastinate or focus our attention elsewhere. It's also normal to feel that the 'brokenness' is just 'who we are,' and so we unwittingly protect it by staying the same. Ultimately, however, this limits both your progress and your potential.

Instead, to change your life for the better, you must choose to develop a healthy self-image that humbly admits to and accepts flaws, while also seeking growth and progress — not sitting in shame, but rather taking ownership and looking forward. The goal is to move past your natural stubbornness and resistance to growth and to step into who you *truly* are.

If you're wondering how long the recovery or healing process will take, the answer is very simple. It will happen when you're ready and willing to let go of your weaknesses and step fully into your true potential.

As Eckhart Tolle said: "All it takes is a simple choice, a simple decision: no matter what happens, **I will create no more pain for myself. I will create no more problems.**"

You Have So Much Potential!

Do you remember the kidnapping scenario at the beginning of this workbook?

As a reminder, imagine you were kidnapped and challenged to stay free from porn and masturbation. The consequence of giving in would be that your entire family is killed.

Clearly, in that scenario, you would be able to summon up the necessary self-control to avoid porn and masturbation at all costs.

So, it IS possible for anyone to stay away from porn. There IS a choice involved, even though it sometimes doesn't feel that way.

Self-control is NOT the issue. Reasons and expectations are.

Unlike climbing a mountain or training for a marathon, when it comes to porn, the choice to not watch it doesn't demand grueling action or effort on your part. It simply requires that you get out of your head, make a clear choice, and not give in to your urges!

Although I strongly advise avoiding triggers and working through the urges in a healthy way, *doing absolutely nothing* is also an option. Why do I say that? Well, *anyone* can choose *not* to watch porn. In fact, **it takes more effort to seek it out and do it, than it does to not.**

Doing nothing is part of your path to freedom. Completing this 30-day challenge does not require any special skills, but it does require a strong desire to quit and a willingness to follow through. I understand it's easier said than done, but it doesn't change the fact that you *do* have the power to succeed. *Everyone* does.

It's important to recognize that you are an eternal being inseparably woven into the fabric of the universe. This is not a mystical claim. It is literal and scientific in every sense. Your intelligence, energy, matter, and history will forever be a part of the universe.

You are important, you are powerful, and your story matters! This infinite nature and interconnection also means you have access to the natural resources and energy the universe provides.

If you are Christian, you can draw power from God, faith, and prayer. If you do not believe in God, there is still harmony, peace, energy, and strength in nature for all those who seek it. There is nothing to hold you back except your own *power to choose*.

The Choice is Yours

Every day I hear things like "I can't," or "What if I fail?" These kinds of comments come from a victim mindset. They are the destructive thoughts that keep people in addiction.

We may not be able to control the weather, gravity, or the choices of others, but we do have the incredible power to choose *how we act.* The principles of agency (exerting personal power of choice) and accountability (accepting ownership over your actions) are incredibly powerful when it comes to addiction recovery. It means first accepting responsibility for your actions and then realizing your personal power to choose.

While the brain of an addict has been altered in a very real, scientifically proven way, you still possess the power of choice. Even though addictive urges may feel unbearable and even compulsive at times, there *are* always other options which we'll discuss in detail in this book. Those options, however, are still dependent on your personal willingness to *choose* them.

While you may feel like a victim to urges and intrusive thoughts, you are not a victim to the addiction itself. In fact, you are reading this because you are *actively seeking* to make better choices and improve. That means you are already heading in the right direction! Trust yourself, and push forward. Again, the reality is, addiction, just like recovery, is yours to choose. You *do* have the power to succeed.

Your Expectations Determine Your Future

> *It is not the highest bar you set, but rather the lowest bar that you allow which defines who you become. Ideals mean nothing until it is no longer an option for you to be less — until you force yourself to honor them. Demand better of yourself and you will be better.*

My house isn't always *clean*, but it is never messier than I allow. Why? Because when the mess hits my threshold for *what's acceptable*, I clean up. Although we may sometimes do things we consider "bad," we rarely do things we consider "unacceptable" (like poisoning your neighbor's dog or lighting your boss's office on fire, however tempting that might feel).

It's similar to addiction. We all have levels of behavior ranging from good to unacceptable, and those expectations guide our lives and choices. Part of the path to recovery then involves changing your expectations, so you can change your life.

According to the noted author John C. Maxwell, the process of change follows this sequence:

Thoughts > Beliefs > Expectations > Attitude >
Behavior > Performance > Your Life

We will develop each one of these in this program.

"Weak Brain"

As I said at the start, you deserve high praise for wanting to quit. You are standing out from the crowd in a positive way and I applaud you for that! There's no doubt that we're living in an *epidemic of porn*. In a way, you should take comfort from this fact though. You are not a freak. You are not a bad person. Yes, you may have developed the habit of regularly looking at porn, but now you're taking action to *stop*.

It's not always that easy though is it? One minute you might have clarity and determination to quit, something shifts, and suddenly you're questioning recovery again. This complicated and frustrating cycle of relapse and recovery can be described as a tug-of-war between two different parts of your brain: your "sober brain" and your "weak brain." Your "sober brain" wants to quit while your "weak brain" craves the addiction.

Science Connection: According to Paul MacLean's 'Triune Brain' model, we really have three "brains."

1. The reptilian or primal brain (basal ganglia) which is responsible for many our instinctual behaviors and developed habits

2. The paleomammalian or emotional brain (limbic system) or our emotional center

3. And the neo-mammalian or rational brain (neocortex)

Addiction relapses occur when we leave our rational brain and enter these "weaker brains" of instinct/habit or emotional reasoning.

While in a sober mindset, you are motivated and disciplined. This is where you tend to operate most of the time. Then, suddenly it seems, the triggers, hormones, stress, and urges build up, and you start questioning your goals. The next thing you know, you've done something you regret. The problem here is that your "weak brain" isn't fully convinced on quitting, and it makes poor decisions that are contrary to your higher goals. To quit, *even your weakest self must be on board.*

There are many things you can do to strengthen your "weak brain.". The most important thing, however, is to be able to identify when you're in a compromised state of mind. Think of it like driving while under the influence. Because of the high risks and consequences of a DUI, most adults recognize when they are too drunk to drive and leave the keys alone.

Likewise, **the decision to watch pornography or masturbate is a serious decision with very real consequences.** Because of this, it's a decision that should only be made in a sober mindset, and not simply because you're experiencing urges.

Your goal is to stay focused on the next 30-days. On day 30, you will make an assessment and re-evaluate how you want to proceed. Before then, however, **your mission** is to keep going, always being aware of your key motivating reason to quit.

Fight or Flight Mode

"Addiction isn't about substance — you aren't addicted to the substance; you are addicted to the alteration of mood that the substance brings." — Susan Cheever

One of the most common reasons individuals turn to pornography, masturbation, and other addictions *is an a*ctivation of an acute stress response, also known as "fight or flight mode." Whenever we are faced with difficult situations, our bodies release hormones that either prepare us to flee the situation (flight) or face it (fight). Addictive impulses, thoughts of suicide, and feeling the urge to "run away" or "check out" are all examples of an *overactive flight response*.

Whether triggered by stress, emotional pain, insecurity, emptiness, or physical discomfort, the porn-masturbation-orgasm cycle (or PMO) seems like an *easy out*. It provides a quick emotional escape and change of mood. However, when you run away from stress rather than facing challenges calmly and confidently, you lose time, focus, and other opportunities for growth and success.

But it gets worse! Repeatedly using PMO in flight mode and turning to dopamine as an escape also *increases* your stress, and anxiety by furthering the cycle of addiction. It also fuels the feelings of shame and guilt that come from viewing pornography.

Of course, the negative, longer-term, consequences of PMO far outweigh any temporary relief, but it can be hard to think clearly and realize that in the moment. Therefore, much of what we will cover in this book is related to regulating emotions.

Testosterone & Hormone Cycles

Men:

Oh yes! Men have "a cycle" too, and understanding your testosterone cycle is critical for your success. That's because most relapses occur on or just before a peak day in the cycle. From my observation as a coach and in speaking with hundreds of men on this issue, the most frequent days when a relapse occurs are weekends (for all addictions) and days 4, 7, and 21 of a streak. Once you understand your body's cycle, you'll be able to plan accordingly and make better decisions.

There are two main testosterone cycles of which you should be aware.

The first is the 7-day cycle. At about seven days post ejaculation, a man's testosterone peaks, creating symptoms of horniness, frustration, or feeling more on edge. On days 5 and 6, leading up to it, one can expect increased urges, energy, frustration, and/or sexual thoughts. The second cycle is a 20-22 day cycle similar to a woman's menstrual cycle. Both the 7-day and 21-day cycles have similar symptoms, with an increase in testosterone.

Knowing this allows you to plan and stay committed in the days that are particularly challenging. If you say to yourself, "It's a peak day, I'm not thinking clearly," you are far more likely to push forward and stay disciplined.

Women:

Women's hormone cycles can also affect their mood and urges. A woman tends to have the highest urges around day 14 of her menstrual cycle (where day 1 is the first day of bleeding,) and again during the days of premenstrual syndrome which is before her next period. This cycle can influence emotional stability and influence any addiction, not just sexual ones.

Preparing for Withdrawals

Before getting started, you need to fully accept the inconvenience and discomfort of the withdrawals you'll go through.

Although everyone is different, in the coming weeks, you will likely feel more tense, frustrated, short tempered, tired, distracted, and anxious while battling urges. Physical discomfort such as increased sensitivity and pressure is also normal. Although it's best to try to relieve your symptoms in healthy ways, and you'll learn many tools for handling urges, be aware that experiencing some discomfort as a result of the addiction is to be expected.

By accepting this beforehand, however, you'll be more mentally prepared and better manage your expectations. Although unpleasant, it's nothing you can't bear. Discomfort never killed anyone, and you *can* get through this, just as countless others already have. Recovery from any addiction involves enduring some withdrawal symptoms, though, and the first few weeks are the hardest. But remember, a few weeks of hardship are nothing compared to the *years of benefits that await you in the future.*

I like to look at it like breaking a wild horse. You've probably seen this in a movie. The horse always bucks heavily in the beginning, but after a while, it tires, and the rider can control it. It's similar with urges. They are always worse in the beginning, but they usually start diminishing after 1-2 weeks. That means, if you stick it out, things **will** get better! On the other hand, if you continue to relapse in the 1-2 week range, you'll continue experiencing the worst symptoms, over and over. That's a powerful incentive in itself to break past that barrier! Most importantly, you must be ready to prioritize your *motivating reason* and your *end goal* OVER your temporary discomfort.

Before beginning, ask yourself the following:

Ask yourself, "Am I prepared and willing to go through some intense physical withdrawals in exchange for the freedom of recovery?" Note your response below.

_____

_____

_____

How much time (in hours/days/weeks/months) am I willing to endure this discomfort before I give in?

_____

PREPARING TO QUIT

This chapter is all about **preparing to quit,** and it's extremely important. I'm sure you're anxious to get going, but diving in unprepared is the reason most people struggle with relapse, so next we'll look at properly preparing a game plan for success.

Quitting any addiction is difficult and comes with a lot of mental and physical challenges. There will be days that test you to your very core, and it's important that you **prepare properly in advance,** so you can stand up to the tests. This means taking time to mentally prepare for your recovery, rather than rushing into it.

Preparation involves recognizing the difficulty and magnitude of what you are taking on. It is a humbling and solemn process.

Your attitude should be like someone who is preparing to embark on a long and dangerous trek along steep, unfamiliar terrain, versus casually or excitedly accepting a challenge.

It's vitally important that you recognize the difficulties ahead, as well as the great significance of what you are doing. The more serious you are about preparation, the more likely you are to reach your goal.

Proper preparation includes the following:

- Explore all your doubts, fears, and questions
- Solidify your motivating reasons for quitting
- Decide if you are ready for the required sacrifices

- Check your mental and emotional engine by making sure you have the stamina and 'fuel' for the journey that lies ahead

- Observe and understand the main triggers that affect you. Write them down, and decide in advance how you'll avoid them, when possible.

- Ponder who you want to be and how you want to FEEL about yourself. What will it feel like when you accomplish your goal? How will that affect your personal and professional life?

Be sure to take time to study, meditate, and journal on each of the points above. The more you're mentally prepared, the greater your likelihood of success. DO NOT RUSH IT. You do not need to have all the answers right now, but don't skip this important phase of the process. Remember, if you fail to plan, you plan to fail!

Make the Decision to Quit

As a reminder, to quit successfully, you must decide to do just that! Addiction rewires the brain, but that doesn't mean you are powerless. *Anyone* CAN quit and recover from their addictions if they put their mind to it.

Remember, your brain is incredibly powerful, and *it is profoundly affected both by what you think and say.* You'll need to eliminate excuse phrases like: "I want to recover" or "I should do the 30 days." Even "I hope to" isn't good enough anymore. You must say to yourself "I *am* going to quit." You need to both *want* it and *believe* it's going to happen in order to succeed.

This also means no more saying things like:

- "I hope I don't relapse."
- "I hope I don't mess up."
- "Quitting would be nice."
- "I hope I get through next week."

And instead, start saying things like:

- "I will reach my goal."
- "I AM going to recover."
- "It may be difficult, but I WILL get through this."

In the words of Yoda, as written by George Lucas: "Try not. Do... or do not. **There is no try.**"

Keep your reasons in a highly visible place, repeat them to yourself often, meditate on them, and visualize yourself succeeding.

GAME PLAN

"By failing to prepare, you are preparing to fail." — Benjamin Franklin

"It does not do to leave a live dragon out of your calculations if you live near one." - J.R.R. Tolkien

"Give me six hours to chop down a tree, and I will spend the first four sharpening the axe." — Abraham Lincoln

Before jumping into your commitments and goals, you need to have a solid plan. Why? Because without a plan, you're setting yourself up for failure. Would an army go into battle without a strategy? Of course not! So, let's look at the components of a good plan:

- An exit strategy
- Correctly set goals
- A way to take care of yourself
- A list of distraction activities
- People you can connect with
- A primary accountability/support person
- A list of triggers to remove/block

- A specific time for meditation/introspection each day
- Goals for other relevant lifestyle changes for your success

In your game plan, it's important to have a toolkit of distractions and soothing activities for managing the mental and physical effects of withdrawal. One of the worst mistakes you can make is choosing to simply "suffer through" urges rather than taking care of yourself in a healthy way. Sometimes it's all you can do, but it's far better to try to satisfy the urge in new and healthy ways if possible.

COPING WITH URGES

When you experience urges, physical or mental, they can be difficult to cope with and resist. It's important to remember, however, that in the first few weeks of recovery, the majority of urges are just symptoms of *addiction* and will reduce over time.

When we look at combatting urges, short and long term, the process includes three parts: preventing, addressing, and re-wiring. In the next few sections we will cover these and many practical ways to handle urges.

Re-Routing Sexual Energy

Feeling an excess of energy or feeling "sexually charged" is one type of sexual urge leading to the temptation of relapse or other poor choices. The best way to handle these urges is to take that energy and apply it to something physical. Often an activity such as running, weightlifting, yoga, boxing, or even just a vigorous walk or doing some yard work will do the trick. When the urge is caused by an emotional need (connection, affirmation, validation, a break, etc.) focus on filling that need in a healthy way. For example, you could spend time with friends, do some self-care, journal, etc.

It's important to remember to do what works for *you*. I coach a lot of men who enjoy going to the gym and can lift harder on peak days. For others though, the gym is too triggering, and they avoid it on those days. There's no right or wrong solution here except to do what works for *you*. Also, keep trying new things. If something is not working, simply try something else until you find something that works for you.

Here's some suggestions:

- Get out of the house
- Spoil yourself with a treat
- Do a physical activity
- Enjoy nature
- Read a book
- Clean a closet
- Start an art project
- Go for a walk or run
- Go to the gym
- Watch some clean comedy, a documentary, a movie, TV, etc.
- Learn a new skill or hobby
- Do a puzzle or play a game
- Take a cold shower
- Perform yoga
- Meditate and focus on breathing
- Exercise / stretching
- Dance
- Sleep
- Talk to a family member or friend

Remember, **there's no need to be afraid of failure when you have a plan.**

Finding Contentment

Another strategy to deal with urges is to practice finding peace and contentment with your body. Our brains are programmed to act on urges, but if you are practicing abstinence, urges are the end. That's as far as you go. Fantasizing will only leave you feeling frustrated or push you closer to giving in, Instead, if you see urges as an ending rather than a trigger, you will be less likely to act on them.

Finding sexual contentment during seasons of abstinence does not mean denying your sexual nature, but rather taking a rain check on the full experience. Sexuality is a deeply personal form of self-expression and an integral part of who you are. Trying to eliminate that part of you is damaging and isn't necessary for your abstinence. Rather than feeling frustrated or giving in to urges, choose to be at peace. Choose to settle your mind and heart. That way, you can experience the urges for what they are without perpetuating them or feeling guilty. Allow them to exist, to pass through you, and to fade away. It's okay to want those things, but it's not okay to act on them or to tease yourself.

Remember, healthy abstinence is not choking your sexuality, but bridling it.

Exit Strategy

Can you think of a time you did something wrong, knowing full well you should quit or leave the situation? Maybe it was a time you were relapsing and heard a voice in the back of your mind saying you should stop, but you didn't have the strength. Why was it so hard to make the right choice? Why did you continue doing something you knew was wrong while arguing with your conscience?

This is where having an exit strategy comes in. Now, it may seem counterintuitive to talk about how to stop yourself while messing up, when the goal is to not mess up, but stay with me on this.

What is an exit strategy? It's anything you do or think to signal to your "weak brain" that it's time to listen. It can be saying a safe word to pull yourself out of the trance or a simple strategy like counting to three. It can be gently snapping your wrist with a rubber band that you are wearing as a bracelet. You may even be able to incorporate your key motivating reason into the plan and have an exit strategy that helps you to remember your priorities.

When in the process of a relapse, oftentimes people deceive themselves, saying things like, "I'm already halfway there" or they simply put off the right decision until it's too late. Your exit strategy, therefore, is designed to make the process of backing out and redirecting easier. It is your last resort, but that also means it's the most crucial. Think of it as a last line of defense to prevent failure.

During my time in college, I remember times when I was in situations that troubled me, but I felt too uncomfortable to tell my friends or leave. Even more challenging are sexually arousing situations. Hormones take over, and it can feel like you're in a trance, with part of your mind saying "stop," but you simply don't feel up to it. That's the purpose of an exit strategy — to bridge that gap between your "sober brain" and your "weak brain" and snap you out of doing something you'll later regret.

As you can see, it's important to plan your exit strategy *before* the situation arises, that way you will be properly prepared.

Here are a few examples and ideas:

- Count to 3, take a deep breath, and then stop what you are doing and leave the situation.

- Create a "safe word" with yourself that means stop immediately (an emergency break so to speak).

- Decide on a distraction that forces you to pause, before deciding if you want to continue and go through with what you're doing (e.g. 30 pushups, a cold shower, Bible study, 5 mins of meditation).

- Decide on a simple phrase that gives you either a polite way to leave or to turn down offers if other people are present

What exit strategies appeal to you?

Once you've tried an exit strategy or been in a situation of temptation again, did it help? If not, why? What happened? What were your thoughts? What can you do differently next time? It's a process of learning and implementing different ideas until you find what works for you.

_____

_____

_____

_____

Reset Strategy

You'll also need what I call a "Reset Strategy." This is what you'll use in moments when you're not necessarily doing anything you need to stop, but you're thinking about it. Let's say it's eyeing a woman/man in a lustful way. In those first moments, you're still in control of yourself, so that's when you need to take decisive, positive action with a strategy that immediately resets your brain to become *sober* again.

Consider a situation you've probably experienced: You're on a video call or Zoom meeting with someone to whom you're really attracted. You need to pay attention to what the person is saying, but the sexual thoughts are overwhelming you. You can barely focus. You need to reset and refocus (not to mention getting that awkward smile off your face before they notice).

The strange thing about this situation is that even when you are trying to stop, it often feels like you can't. The dialogue in your head is bouncing between thoughts of physical gratification and "stop, and pay attention." Meanwhile, your excitement keeps building.

Now, say an armed burglar suddenly walks into your room, shouting and making threats at you. How would your thoughts change? Instantly, right?! You might be startled with a quick gasp of air, as your focus shifts to the urgent threat in front you. You immediately snap out of those previous thoughts. The trigger is still in the room, and your hormones haven't changed. So, what's the difference?

The burglar triggered a sense of urgency that slapped you out of that shallow mindset.

The good news is that with practice, you can take control of your thoughts. Like a muscle that requires you to use it consistently to make it stronger, practicing a reset strategy will become easier with time.

The first step is cultivating the right desire to change your thoughts when needed. You *must* have a compelling reason. Maybe it's your religious beliefs, a desire to view people on a deeper level, or maybe you simply want to develop better mental control. It takes a lot of mental maturity and control, but it's very possible.

Practice the following steps when you are struggling with lustful thoughts:

1. When you are in a moment of temptation and decide you want to stop, start by taking a deep cleansing breath.

2. Admit your behavior is going in the wrong direction and that you'll have to change and let go in order to be who you **want to be.**

3. Decide who you *really* want to be, and own it.

What does a mature, respectful, and mentally powerful person look like to you?

_____

_____

_____

Now, think of a few good reasons to avoid lustful thoughts, and record them here:

_____

_____

_____

Removing Triggers

To be effective, you must remove triggers wherever possible.

Triggers can be any person, place, thing, thought, behavior, or activity that prompts you to crave or think about your addiction.

Triggers can be external or internal, and it's important to learn to identify which ones affect you. Triggers include things like social media, apps, movies, TV shows, and even friends that are influencing your addiction or hindering you from reaching your goals. If anything, or anyone is bringing you down, and you know it, set a date, get tough with yourself, and say goodbye. The initial sacrifice may be hard, but I assure you the benefits will outweigh the loss.

What triggers can you identify and remove to boost your success?

_____

_____

_____

_____

Accountability and Consequences

Consequences and accountability partners can be extremely helpful in completing this challenge. In fact, many recovered addicts say that confiding in a friend is the most helpful tool in their recovery.

Yes, it's a hard conversation to have, but if you choose your accountability partner wisely, they will be happy to support you in your goal. They'll constantly be on the sidelines cheering you on. Step out of the shadow of shame, and take the bold step of confiding in someone you respect and trust. You won't regret it.

One of the most inventive, personal strategies for overcoming PMO I've heard was created by a friend. One day he came to me and said, "Heather, I'm going to pay you $5 if I masturbate and $10 if I watch porn. I know it will be too embarrassing for me to tell you, and I'm too broke to pay you. I always keep my word though, so I won't have any choice." After several months, he relapsed on masturbation only once and handed me $5. That was the last time he masturbated during his 30-day recovery program. The accountability and the consequence he established outweighed his urges to give up.

When you establish your system of accountability and consequence, look for an accountability partner who:

- will be honest and tough.
- will love you unconditionally and won't be ashamed of you.
- won't be emotionally hurt by your relapse.
- will be available to give you time and attention in critical moments.

When establishing consequences for yourself make sure they:

- do not deprive you of needed self-care.
- do not hurt you or anyone else.
- don't lead to self-shaming.

Describe your plan for consequences or accountability during the next 30 days:

_____

_____

_____

_____

_____

Weaning

What is weaning? Weaning is a medical term that describes the process of slowly reducing the use of a drug to ease the symptoms of withdrawal. It can also be applied to sexual addiction.

Some people believe that the process of weaning makes it easier for them to recover from a porn and masturbation addiction. However, it's definitely a double-edged sword because weaning invariably leads to experiencing withdrawal symptoms over a longer period of time, as well as a slower recovery.

The choice is yours, and only you know what your body can handle. Here are a few simple suggestions:

- Don't wean if you don't have to. Giving up masturbation altogether is typically better.

- Establish your plan BEFORE starting, otherwise you may be tempted to use weaning as an excuse for a relapse.

- If you have been masturbating every day, or multiple times a day, and this is your first shot at quitting, you may try a simple 4 days, 5 days, 8 days, and then progress to 30 days. These numbers are strategic, don't change them.

- Note: The above plan is for masturbation only. There is no excuse for relapse on porn and no exceptions.

REWIRING YOUR BRAIN

You may have heard that porn and other addictions "rewire your brain." It's true, but *how* does that happen, and what should you *do* about it? Each of the activities in this book are designed to *rewire* different parts of your brain, and guide you through the process of recovery.

After years of consuming toxic, pornographic material and the resulting cycles of guilt, shame, secrecy, and insecurity, recovery may feel overwhelming. This is just another effect of porn. Mentally, pornography "rewires" your thoughts, perspectives, expectations, and emotions.

The process of long-term recovery will involve shifting these perspectives and developing positive habits of *thought*. Learning to believe in yourself, to forgive yourself, to take ownership of your life, and to view sexuality in a healthier way are all *critical to your success.* We'll dig deeper into these in coming sections with specific strategies.

1. Re-Framing: Porn is NOT Helpful

One of the most common causes for relapse is viewing porn as a tool for success. Examples of these thoughts include:

1. "I'm horny and can't focus. Masturbation will help."
2. "I'm frustrated with my family/ girlfriend/ co-workers. Porn will help."
3. "I need porn to calm down before bed."
4. "I don't want a relationship. Porn will help me not want/need women"

If you view porn, or other addictions, as a *tool* for coping with life, the logical choice will be relapse. It's a no brainer. If you believe "porn = success," you will continue to choose the porn.

However, if you reframe it, and recognize that **addiction** is the **cause** of many of your unwanted symptoms, quitting becomes the most logical decision even in times of difficult urges. The way you think dictates your actions. Change your thoughts and you will change your life.

Remember: Porn is NOT a tool for success.

2. Leverage Dopamine

Next up, is the physical re-wiring of porn and sexual addiction caused by the hormone dopamine, the "reward and pleasure hormone."

When you train a dog, there are three basic steps: *trigger, action, and reward.* First, you give it a command, and if it obeys the command, you give it a treat, which makes it happy. It's exactly the same process with addiction. When you feel an urge or see a trigger and act on it, you get a "reward" of dopamine. The process of re-rewiring is similar, but this time when you experience a trigger, you perform a **new** action, to get a new reward.

This is a simple concept, it's just not always *easy*. Let's look at it further.

When you experience a physical urge, there is a moment of choice: you can give in to the urge, or do something else. When you choose a NEW action (e.g., going to the gym) followed by a new reward (e.g., a shake afterwards), you begin to rewire the addiction and your response to those triggers.

Trigger > Decision to not use PMO > New action > New reward

Keep in mind that you'll want to have different options for alternative activities for different times. For example, going for a run isn't practical at midnight, so you need to think of alternatives for different circumstances. In an upcoming module, you will write out and practice a variety of activities for when you experience triggers.

3. Use Rewards

Rewards, though often overlooked, are an important part of your recovery!

> "Almost everything will work again if you unplug it for a few minutes, including you." — Anne Lamott

> "Keep good company, read good books, love good things and cultivate soul and body as faithfully as you can." — Louisa May Alcott

> "The care, therefore, of every man's soul belongs unto himself." — John Locke

Rewards and pleasure are integral parts of life that motivate us and make us happy. For example, if I were to ask an alcoholic: "What do you do when you're happy?" They'd most likely say, "I like to drink." If I asked them, "What do you do when you're sad?" they will likely respond, "I like to drink." That's because drinking has become their primary reward system, and they have developed a toxic dependency on it.

A lot of people are familiar with the advice "find a distraction to take your mind off your addiction." This strategy tends to be ineffective. The reason distraction alone often fails is because it's missing the final, and key component: **the reward.**

If a person simply 'pushes through' urges by staying busy with work, for example, it could lead to serious burnout or a binge down the road. What a person really needs after a long day is not more work, but rather a relaxing and comforting *reward*. They need to take care of themselves and their needs, not push harder.

In some cases, the reward can be the distraction activity, but the new reward is the critical piece that can't be skipped.

Examples of rewards:

- Enjoy your favorite food
- Order takeout
- Watch a game
- Enjoy a TV show
- Watch some clean comedy
- Buy yourself something nice
- Plan a trip or outing
- Start or continue a hobby
- Go on a hike or spend time in nature
- Do something new
- Change your routine to make it fun
- "Give" yourself extra time or money to do something special
- Take a day or evening off

Be aware and mindful that any of these activities can also become an unhealthy addiction on their own when taken to the extreme of indulgence, so it's your responsibility to choose healthy rewards wisely. Balance is the key.

Now, many people find the concept of "rewards" to be difficult to apply. Some feel they already "get whatever they want when they want it," and others simply can't think of any rewards. Part of the problem here is they do not know themselves well enough due to the addiction and the rewiring of their brain that has occurred. They are unable to clearly define things that make them happy.

If you are struggling with this, you are not alone. It is important though that you take establishing a new reward system seriously. You **deserve** and **need** healthy rewards!

4. Distraction Activities:

When battling urges, distractions are another simple but effective tool for staying focused on recovery and rewiring your brain. As a part of your Game Plan, write down some ideas to prepare in advance for the following scenarios. Here are a few examples

- Go to the gym
- Work
- Start a project
- Hike/walk
- Visit a friend
- Perform a service activity
- Learn a skill
- Participate in a favorite hobby
- Read self-development books
- Exercise
- Listen to podcasts
- Read and engage in the Fight The Beast Member portal

Which distraction activities and rewards appeal to you? Feel free to include your own!

When you're tired:

Distraction activity: _____

Reward: _____

When you're at home:

Distraction activity: _____

Reward: _____

When you're away from home:

Distraction activity: _____

Reward: _____

When you go to bed or wake up:

Distraction activity: _____

Reward: _____

YOUR RELATIONSHIP WITH GOD

"The Lord never tires of forgiving. It is we who tire of asking forgiveness."
— Pope Francis

'[God's love] is not wearied by our sins, or our indifference; and, therefore, it is quite relentless in its determination that we shall be cured of those sins, at whatever cost to us, at whatever cost to Him." — CS Lewis

"For God so loved the world, that he gave his only begotten Son, that whosoever believeth in him should not perish, but have everlasting life. For God sent not his Son into the world to condemn the world; but that the world through him might be saved." — John 3:16

Though Fight The Beast is a non-religious, non-denominational organization, I would be remiss for not dedicating a portion of this book to God and the powerful role faith plays in the recovery of millions. Although I won't go into much depth regarding faith and God in this version of the program, here are a few thoughts that might enhance your journey to recovery and your walk with God or a higher being:

- God's love is perfect and infinite. Nothing you can do can change His love.

- You are His child and have divine nature and potential.

- He is intimately aware of your struggle and wants to see you become strong through the refiner's fire and the process of recovery.

- Unfortunately, God will not always remove the *consequences* of our actions, including the consequences of addiction. As a parent, He seems to say, "I told you over and over. I warned you not to get tangled in sin because I knew it would hurt and be as a *cord around your neck*. Nevertheless, I will forgive you and walk with you on the journey home."

- Christ's Atonement, forgiveness, and grace is infinite — in depth and breadth. You are never too far gone. And no mistake is too "bad" for His forgiveness and healing power.

- Christ died not to judge or shame us, but so that we could be forgiven and justified. Christ died for YOU so YOU could be forgiven. What an incredible gift of love. Accept it graciously!

- Finally, prayer and fasting are great tools for recovery for added strength from temptation and urges. Consider Matthew 17:21: "Howbeit this kind [of evil spirit] goeth not out but by prayer and fasting."

As you walk this road, I encourage you to have faith and look to the future with hope and optimism. You are on the right path — the same path walked by even King David, a chosen man of God, after he fell to lust and sexual sin. Your sins are known by God, but He has offered you forgiveness.

Furthermore, try to remember that although He loves you, forgives you, and wants you to be happy, He also wants you to **grow**. Just like a child learning to walk, He sees the value in your stumbling. He is watching as you continue to fight, push forward, and stand back up from your falls. It is all a part of the process of becoming strong and reaching the potential He sees in you!

Just like addiction can block your ability to feel love from and for others, it can also block and limit your spiritually. If you are struggling to feel, hear, or see God's hand in your life, just know that this veil will lift as you continue faithfully down the path of recovery. As your spirituality increases, you will struggle less and vice versa.

In fact, this veil lifting is so powerful, that I have even received letters from former atheists that found God in recovery. One such letter explained, "As I got clean from pornography, I began to feel God's presence more and more in my life until it became undeniable. I just couldn't connect with Him before because of my addiction and the sin I was in."

As you continue the journey of recovery, you may use the following space to record your impressions regarding God, His love for you, His plan for your life, forgiveness, grace, and other thoughts and scriptures that come to you:

_____

_____

_____

_____

_____

_____

_____

FREQUENTLY ASKED QUESTIONS

If I relapse should I keep going or start over? After completing the relapse section, just keep going! You may even skip ahead to topics that you relate to or feel you need.

How long will recovery take? Recovery is a process that starts *today*. If you choose to keep yourself clean *today* congratulations! If you relapse and learn from your relapse, you are still *one step closer* to full recovery. You will first focus on reaching 7 days and then 30 days. How long it takes you is up to you!

The more consistent and diligent you are with this book and participation in our online community, the more successful you'll be!

Should I tell my partner / spouse about my addiction? This program is different because we don't necessarily recommend involving your partner. For some it may be helpful, and if you feel strongly about telling your partner then you should! However, as a woman once married to a partner struggling with sex addiction, I can tell you that it can be extremely difficult for your partner to emotionally process. Alternatively, I suggest finding an accountability partner that is not as emotionally connected to your relapses or recovery process.

Will this increase my risk of prostate cancer? No! In fact, it can even reduce your risk. According to the famous Harvard study on ejaculation and prostate cancer risk, 4-7 ejaculations a month has increased risk compared to 21+ times a month, however, less also has a decreased risk. In addition, young men in their teens and 20s can increase their risk of erectile dysfunction and prostate cancer from high consumption of porn and masturbation. Furthermore, studies show that diet, exercise, and genetics play a higher role in prostate cancer risk. So, don't worry! Your risk is minimal, but more importantly this will benefit your life in so many other aspects, it's worth it!

Will my testicles change size? It's a legitimate question! The short answer is we don't have a ton of research on this, but we do have reports from the hundreds of men in our community. It seems that testicle sizes decrease as semen production decreases; however, testicle size seems to increase to their normal size after some time.

What if I'm leaking? The first week or two is usually the hardest. During this time, your semen production will still be high, but your release amount has come to a screeching halt. Leaking is a result of this over production, but it will resolve over time.

Are "wet dreams" relapse? "Wet dreams" or nocturnal emission is your body's natural way of secreting old fluids and "cleaning the pipes". Although it may reset some aspects of your body and hormone clock, you don't need to feel guilty about them unless you intentionally did something to trigger it. If you would like to avoid sexual dreams, you can also try a new bed time routine and meditation before bed.

David Haye, the heavyweight boxing champion, once spoke on his determination to avoid even wet dreams saying, "Find a lion that hasn't had some food for a while, and you've got a dangerous cat. So, there won't be a drip from me. Even in my sleep — if there are girls all over me in my dream, I say to them, 'I've got a fight next week, I can't do anything. I can't do it.' That's control."

What is flatline? Why do I feel numb? Did something break? Around 30-45 days of abstinence, it's not uncommon for men to suddenly feel numb and have no urges. We call this a flatline. This can cause a lot of men to relapse worried that they no longer have a sex drive or that something "broke." Rest assured, nothing broke. Your body is just giving you a much-needed break from the urges! You will likely get urges back within a few weeks. It's also important to remember that NOT having random urges that aren't associated with love is a good thing. That's your goal — to not be triggered by random things!

Should I have sex? This one is difficult to answer generically because there are a lot of factors involved. Many men find it helpful to practice complete abstinence in their first 30 days or even periodically thereafter. Some men choose to stay sexually active. Here is some guidance on when to abstain completely: If you are married or in a committed relationship, having sex can be normal UNLESS: 1) you notice increased aggravation towards your partner, 2) having sex is triggering heavier urges, 3) you are using your partner excessively to satisfy addictive urges instead of emotionally connecting. Furthermore, I do not recommend casual sex for any reason during this process.

I have a fetish. Will quitting help? Yes. Total abstinence and rewiring of your brain can help with unwanted fetishes. As you learn to connect love with sex, things will improve!

Will this help with erectile dysfunction? Yes. Many of our members experience the reversal of Porn Induced Erectile Dysfunction from recovery. By the 21-day testosterone peak, your body has been reset and is ready to go!

Final Miscellaneous Tips

- **Food and/or drink fasting:** Many men report a decrease in urges when fasting.

- **Better sleep routine and natural sleeping aids:** Urges can be difficult especially around bedtime. A healthy bedtime routine of relaxing activities, avoiding blue light, going to bed early, chamomile or other relaxing herbal teas, and even a natural sleeping aid can help.

- **Charge your phone away from your bedroom:** Many relapses occur in the early and late hours of the day when your mind isn't fully conscious. Keeping your phone in another room will help prevent drowsy decision making that could lead to watching porn.

- **Healthy diet:** Diet can influence urges significantly. Maintaining a healthy diet while avoiding sugar and hormone disruptors can help.

- **Testosterone pills:** Unless you have a very specific medical reason for taking testosterone pills, we recommend putting them on hold as they will increase urges. The process of recovery and the healthy habits explained in this program will naturally boost your testosterone, motivation, and healthy sex drive anyway.

- **Software filters & porn blockers:** Filters and blocking apps can be really helpful in restricting and preventing watching impromptu sexual content.

- **Clean media:** From social media to music, the entertainment and media you can consume can be a huge trigger. Many men find it helpful to avoid sexual, lewd, violent, and even romantic content during recovery and after.

- **Exercise:** Burning off urges and sexual energy through exercise and fitness is also really helpful. Not only will it reduce urges, but it will help you sleep better too!

Time to Commit!

Set Reasonable Goals And Never Break Them

It's finally time to make your first **commitment** for recovery and get started!

More often than not, relapse comes in the form of "changing your mind". So instead of setting a traditional "goal," I suggest *re-evaluation dates*. A revaluation day is different from a goal because it restricts your *decision making* to a specific time and day. **It is a commitment to not change your mind.** Only when you successfully reach that day/time can you decide to quit, **BUT NOT BEFORE**. This will increase your discipline and keep you focused, while still giving you the "option" to change your mind in the future, but only **AFTER** you reach the date.

The benefit here is that not only are you more likely to reach your goal with this technique, but it gives you time to experiment and watch for all potential benefits or drawbacks. Plus, pushing through the difficult times will help you become stronger and more disciplined.

Of course, if you are completely sure you will *never* have the desire or urge to watch porn *ever* again and you have absolutely *no* risk for changing your mind, then this might not apply to you. However, most readers won't fall in that category and will benefit from this type of commitment and goal setting during recovery.

To set this type of goal, you might say to yourself:

> "I will not change my mind until (date) _____. However, **only** when I reach my Re-Evaluation Day, will I decide if I want to continue or quit."

This works wonders in preventing premature quitting! Be sure to always set a reachable goal though. Getting burnt out or overwhelmed is the quickest route to failure. Set a goal that pushes you, but that you feel comfortable committing to, and be sure it is specific and well documented.

Then, whatever you do, don't give in or change your mind until the end. Seeing the goal all the way through is the most important piece and an important sacrifice worth making *for your relationship with yourself,* your confidence, and the process of building discipline.

Final Step for SUCCESS:

Now, you've finally reached the end of our introduction! With these principles and tools, you're more prepared than ever to reach your goals and stay clean!

It's time to start your first 7 days (or another 7 days clean if you're already practicing abstinence), but first, review and finalize your game plan on the following page!

MY GAME PLAN

Write your plan for each of the following.

My commitment: "I will not change my mind or relapse until at LEAST (date) _____. However, when I reach my Re-Evaluation Day, I can decide if I want to continue or quit."

My powerful, motivating reason:

_____

_____

My exit and/or reset strategy:

_____

_____

The healthy way I plan to take care of myself:

_____

_____

Distraction activities I will use:

_____

_____

_____

Names of people I can connect with/ reach out to:

_____

_____

My accountability/support person:

_____

_____

Possible triggers I have or will remove/block:

_____

_____

_____

My specific time for meditation/introspection each day:

_____

_____

_____

Other lifestyle changes I want to make that will promote success:

_____

_____

_____

Section 2

Overcoming Relapse

BEFORE READING. This section is meant to help you analyze and process relapses if and when you experience them. If you just set your first commitment, skip to Section 3 and begin your first 7 days! Come back to this section only as needed.

This Is A Shame Free Zone. Period.

"Success is not final, failure is not fatal: it is the courage to continue that counts. — Winston Churchill

"Be patient with yourself. You are growing stronger every day. The weight of the world will become lighter... and you will begin to shine brighter. Don't give up." — Robert Tew

In the beginning, we discussed creating a shame-free, growth environment for 30 days. That means working towards your goal, without worrying about the past or future. It is important that you give yourself time to grow without the distractions of fear and regret.

Consider the difference between productive guilt and toxic shame. Guilt is an uncomfortable but healthy emotion that helps us recognize what we did wrong, and then motivates us to be better. Shame, on the other hand, is a toxic internal dialogue that keeps you trapped and discouraged.

Below are a few examples of the internal expressions of guilt versus shame:

Productive Guilt

- I shouldn't have done that.
- I need to change.
- I feel bad for doing that.
- I want to be better.
- I need to make up for what I did.

Toxic Shame

- I'm an idiot.
- I'm a horrible person.
- I'm no good.
- I don't deserve love.
- I'll never be good enough.

Activity

If you find yourself in a place of shame versus healthy guilt, try the following:

- *First, do whatever is necessary to clear your conscience. If you have hurt someone else, apologize sincerely. If you feel you ought to confess to God or to your religious leader, it's important that you do so. True repentance involves admitting to a wrong, making restitution, and resolving to improve. In the long run, these steps will free you to move forward with a clean conscience.*

- *Second, forgive yourself. You were a different person when you made the mistake. You are a different person now. It's impossible to change the past, but you should learn from it. Focus on what you learned, why you're changing, and who you want to be in the future.*

- *Third, you can also try repeating positive affirmations that will help you get into the right mindset. For example: "Tomorrow is a new day, I'll do better tomorrow, I'm working on it."*

- *Lastly, don't overthink it. Sometimes we have guilt from unresolved questions that we haven't let go. Some questions don't have answers, and others don't need to be answered. Sometimes the most important answer is "it doesn't matter."*

Write down a specific regret that you have experienced:

_____

_____

What positive outcomes came from that situation or mistake?

How did it help you grow?

What more can you learn from it?

How can you use that experience to benefit yourself or others?

_____

_____

_____

BOUNCING BACK FROM RELAPSE

"Mistakes are part of the game. It's how well you recover from them, that's the mark of a great player." — Alice Cooper

A relapse is the word that describes someone who returns to porn, masturbation, or other addictions after a period of being sober.

A relapse can feel crushing. But guess what? It's not the end of your story. It's not even close to the end. It's vital to keep things in perspective. Just like crashing a car in a video game or watching a movie scene where everything seems to fall apart, it's simply a small moment in your life-long journey.

Look at it this way. As a toddler learning to walk, imagine if the first time you fell over, you said to yourself, "Well, that's it then, it's never going to happen!" Your infant brain then decides to stay rolling around on the comfort of the carpet forever!

Obviously that scenario sounds and is ridiculous! Yet, that's what we're doing if we choose to give up after a relapse. The truth is that we're actually *closer* to our goal than we were before!

Still, a relapse can be both frustrating and disappointing. Maybe you were close to reaching 30 days clean, or perhaps you just barely started your recovery. Either way, you stumbled and that's okay. Recognize that a part of you was not fully ready to quit, and when it showed itself, you relapsed.

If you relapse, follow these 5 steps:

1. Process your guilt or shame properly
2. Stay in the present
3. Avoid the trap of envy or comparing yourself
4. Learn from your mistakes
5. Get re-motivated

Let's fight the beast!

RELAPSE IS FOR LEARNING

Is relapse a failure?

Do I lose my progress?

Do I need to start over?

These are common questions surrounding a relapse and the most important thing to know is: you never "start over." Every day you should be learning, growing, and becoming better. Every day that passes without giving in to urges IS a success. The more successful days you string together, the stronger you'll get and the better your life will become. Even a relapse will provide you with information from which you can grow.

Avoid being paralyzed by a relapse. Choose to use the experience to learn more about yourself, your needs, and your weaknesses. Set yourself up for better success next time. That way, something very positive will come out of a bad situation.

When you relapse, ask yourself these key questions <u>*and be sure to write the*</u>

answers in your journal.

What was I doing just before I slipped up?

_____

_____

_____

What else happened that day that may have contributed to the relapse?

_____

_____

_____

_____

What excuses did I make in my mind?

_____

_____

_____

_____

What addiction recovery principle or action did I forget?

_____

_____

_____

How can I revise my plan?

What should I practice or work on this week, so I don't fail again in the same way?

What unmet needs should I work on?

Additional notes about my relapse:

_____

_____

_____

_____

After addressing what went wrong, it's time to go back and review a) your reason, and b) your game plan. Prepare yourself to start the battle again, with renewed determination.

Just like getting back on the horse as soon as possible after falling off, be determined to quickly renew your goal, and stay carefully focused on the tools and principles of success!

Remember: If you're not learning from each relapse, you're not in active recovery, but as long as you keep learning and growing, you're doing just fine. Relapse is an expected part of the recovery process. Over time, the gap between relapses will grow longer and longer.

Avoid Comparing Yourself

Before you compare yourself to the success (or failures) of others, remember that it doesn't matter how long you've been in the fight, only that you're in it! That's a wonderful thing! This is a personal journey and you're the one who chooses who you want to be, and where it ends. This is about YOUR personal progress, and that's all that matters.

Another pitfall is in comparing yourself to others, or giving weight to others' opinions. By staying intensely focused on your life, your goals, your progress, you can cut out the noise of other opinions.

At the end of the day, you live in your own world, and you have the power to write your own story. You are both the hero and the author of your story. Take ownership of it and let go of unqualified opinions that simply don't matter.

Now, answer the following self-reflection questions:

What specific things or goals do you want for yourself?

_____

_____

_____

_____

_____

Are you willing to put in the work?

_____

_____

_____

_____

Do you tend to compete with others? Explain.

_____

_____

_____

_____

From what you've learned, is comparing yourself to others helpful or hurtful to your progress? Explain.

_____

_____

_____

_____

Who do you believe is judging you?

_____

_____

_____

_____

Here's a beautiful poem that describes the relationship between envy and effort. You may find it helpful to review it and meditate on it.

The Truth About Envy — By Edgar Guest

I like to see the flowers grow,
To see the pansies in a row.
I think a well-kept garden's fine,
And wish that such a one were mine;
But one can't have a stock of flowers,
Unless he digs and digs for hours.
My ground is always bleak and bare;
The roses do not flourish there.
And where I once sowed poppy seeds,

Is now a tangled mass of weeds.
I'm fond of flowers, but admit,
For digging I don't care a bit.
I envy men whose yards are gay,
But never work as hard as they.
I also envy men who own
More wealth than I have ever known.
I'm like a lot of men who yearn,
For joys that they refuse to earn.
You cannot have the joys of work
And take the comfort of a shirk.
I find the man I envy most
Is he who's longest at his post.
I could have gold and roses, too,
If I would work like those who do.

What resonates with you about that poem?

_____

_____

_____

How might envy play a negative role in your recovery?

_____

_____

_____

_____

Section 3

Your First 7 Days

WHAT TO EXPECT: The first 7 days of recovery are the most difficult. Your semen production is high (if you're a man), your urges are high, and it's difficult to stay focused. In the first 7 days, you can expect difficulty sleeping, moodiness, obsessive thoughts, and even swings in energy (for better or worse). All of this is normal, but remember, most of these symptoms only last the first week or two. After that, things improve and you feel better than ever!

A FEW TIPS: Stay focused. Stay consistent. Focus on the benefits and your *reason*. And try to reach 7 days clean as quickly as possible! The more you relapse in the difficult 7-day window, the longer you have to deal with the most annoying and difficult symptoms. I promise you; it will get better!

Day 1 - One Step At A Time

"The journey of a thousand miles begins with one step." — Lao-tzu

"The best thing about the future is that it comes one day at a time." — Abraham Lincoln

"Everybody is looking for instant success, but it doesn't work that way. You build a successful life one day at a time." — Lou Holtz

Congratulations! You've reached an exciting stage in your journey of fighting the beast!

Today is the first official day of your 30-day challenge, and the first step of a new life centered around success and self-improvement. How are you feeling? Optimistic? Nervous? If so, that's understandable. This journey is about taking things one day, one step, at a time!

There are three classic pop culture references I often joke about with our community members. You may be familiar with them.

First, from the 1970 Claymation movie "Santa Claus is Comin to Town":

> *"If you want to change your direction / If your time of life is at hand / Well don't be the rule, be the exception / A good way to start is to stand. Put one foot in front of the other / And soon you'll be walking 'cross the floor / Put one foot in front of the other / And soon you'll be walking out the door."* (Lyrics written by Mickey Rooney)

Second, in the 1991 comedy "What About Bob?", Bill Murray's character, Bob, *is an* almost paralyzed multi-phobic patient. His psychiatrist shares with him the advice:

> *"Baby Steps... It means setting small reasonable goals for yourself one day at a time — one, tiny step at a time. For instance, when you leave this office, don't think about everything you have to do in order to get out*

of the building. Just think of what you must do to get out of this room. And when you get out into the hall, deal with that hall, and so forth."

In the coming scenes, Bob is seen walking around New York City repeating the phrase "baby steps" everywhere he goes. While comical in the film, this is an effective strategy for addiction recovery! Rather than worrying about the long-term challenge or potential difficulties, just focus on today. "It's just one day! Baby steps."

Finally, in the words of J.R.R Tolkien, "It's a dangerous business, Frodo, going out your door. You step onto the road, and if you don't keep your feet, there's no knowing where you might be swept off to." So, enjoy today. Keep your feet on the path, and stay focused!

As a reminder, it's been proven time and time again that your recovery will be much faster and more successful if you connect with the supportive community at FightTheBeast.org. If you haven't done so already, be sure to visit that website now.

Affirmations:

- I made the right choice.
- I am on this journey for a reason.
- The past doesn't matter right now.

DAILY **R**EVIEW

Streak Length: _____ **Days to Goal:** _____ **Did you succeed today?** _____

1. How would you rate your urges on a scale of 0-10? *(Give yourself a pat on the back if they were higher than normal and you still succeeded!)* _____

2. How would you rate your mood on a scale of 0-10? _____

3. How would you rate your energy on a scale of 0-10? _____

4. What else did you succeed in today?

   _____

   _____

5. What can you do better tomorrow?

   _____

   _____

6. What is something for which you are grateful today?

   _____

   _____

7. Progress Notes:

   _____

   _____

   _____

Day 2 - The Biggest Mistake You Can Make

"The primary cause of unhappiness is never the situation but thought about it. Be aware of the thoughts you are thinking. Separate them from the situation, which is always neutral. It is as it is." — Eckhart Tolle

"When you recognize that there is a voice in your head that pretends to be you and never stops speaking, you are awakening out of your unconscious identification with the stream of thinking. When you notice that voice, you realize that who you are is not the voice - the thinker - but the one who is aware of it." — Eckhart Tolle

"The wise treat horniness like a hiccup; the foolish, like an asthma attack."
— Mokokoma Mokhonoana

The biggest mistake you can make is *identifying* with your urges and thoughts. For example, saying things like: "I want," "I'm horny," "I need." Let me explain.

Thoughts and urges happen because of chemicals, which can be triggered by anything from the weather to a fragrance, or even the microbiology of your gut.

The reality is: you are *not* your thoughts or your urges. If you were, you couldn't control them. Right? And think about this: for *most of the time* you are completely committed to quitting. You make plans and fight urges throughout the day. The difference between fighting them and giving in though, is often a matter of *whether you identify with them.*

It's critical you see your urges and thoughts as an *experience*. Allow urges to exist in your body as necessary, but avoid claiming or identifying with them. Simply learn to coexist with the urges, while keeping your deeper goals at the wheel.

Meditation:

Today's meditation practice focuses on taking a break from "thought". The goal is to become **aware** of your thoughts and urges. You will mentally acknowledge they're present, but *disassociate* from them. In a calm, undistracted space, read the following, and then set a 10-minute timer to practice.

Step 1: If you are experiencing strong emotions or physical pain/urges/sensations, try to observe them as if on a TV screen. Try to identify where in your body your thoughts, feelings, or emotions exist. This can take practice, be patient with yourself.

Step 2: Now, begin to clear your mind. Focus on your physical sensations, but avoid thinking about or describing them. Instead, just *feel* them. Your goal is to become like a tree — exist in a natural state without *thinking* about your existence, and to simply feel without thinking about feeling.

Step 3: If you're struggling with sexual urges today, try to be their friend. *Accept their existence* while realizing you don't need to change, release, or arouse them. Allow them to pass through you, but not control you.

Affirmations:

- I am more than my thoughts.
- I am more than my urges.
- I have a special place and role in nature.
- I will successfully complete these 30 days, one day at a time.

DAILY REVIEW

Streak Length: _____   **Days to Goal:** _____   **Did you succeed today?** _____

1. How would you rate your urges on a scale of 0-10? *(Give yourself a pat on the back if they were higher than normal and you still succeeded!)* _____

2. How would you rate your mood on a scale of 0-10? _____

3. How would you rate your energy on a scale of 0-10? _____

4. What else did you succeed in today?
   _____
   _____

5. What can you do better tomorrow?
   _____
   _____

6. What is something for which you are grateful today?
   _____
   _____

7. Progress Notes:
   _____
   _____
   _____

DAY 3 - VISUALIZATION

"Dare to visualize a world in which your most treasured dreams have become true." — Ralph Marston

"To accomplish great things we must first dream, then visualize, then plan... believe... act!" — Alfred A. Montapert

"Visualization is daydreaming with a purpose." — Bo Bennett

As a reminder, visualization is one of the most powerful tools used by successful entrepreneurs, athletes, and others to achieve their goals. It can be a valuable tool for you too.

In one research study, participants were asked to play a sequence of piano notes for five days in a row. One group practiced on a real piano while the other only visualized playing the notes. The amazing thing is that the brain activity and changes recorded over the five-day period were virtually the same for both groups, proving that to the brain, visualization is a *real* experience with *real* outcomes. In other words, the brain perceives a visualization to be *just as real* as the actual activity.

To try this yourself, spend a few minutes in a calm, quiet setting and visualize achieving success in overcoming your porn addiction. Visualize each of the steps to get there. Start by imagining yourself completing this challenge. How does victory feel? How will your life be different?

Also, it's vital to practice good habits like not opening inappropriate content on your device, or choosing distractions and rewards in place of PMO. Thinking through what you'll do *before* a triggering situation arises will help you succeed. Think about how great you'll feel to accomplish this goal!

A warning: Visualization can also be your worst enemy if used improperly. If you *allow* your mind to wander or fantasize (yes, it is a choice), those sexual thoughts *also* create real changes (arousal, semen production, anxiety etc.)

which will result in higher frustration and possibly relapse.

So, to avoid making things harder on yourself, determine right now to let go of all fantasies and arousing thoughts. Yes, they may pop into your head, but you still have a choice whether to feed them further, or instantly reject them. Choose to focus on your success, rather than your temptations, and spend your time visualizing what you *want most* versus what you are trying to *avoid!*

One way to do this is to practice visualizing your success in recovery. You may also practice visualizing yourself turning off devices in temptation or choosing something better to do. This practice will strengthen you immensely to be better equipped to handle urges in the future. After your meditation, record your thoughts below.

Journaling:

What does it feel like to think about your recovered state?

_____

_____

_____

_____

_____

_____

How will you change as a person?

_____

_____

_____

What steps will you take to get there?

Affirmations:

- I can accomplish my goals.
- I can be who I want to be.
- I am doing my best, and that's all that matters.
- I will stay focused on reaching 30 days clean!

Daily Review

Streak Length: _____ **Days to Goal:** _____ **Did you succeed today?** _____

1. How would you rate your urges on a scale of 0-10? *(Give yourself a pat on the back if they were higher than normal and you still succeeded!)* _____

2. How would you rate your mood on a scale of 0-10? _____

3. How would you rate your energy on a scale of 0-10? _____

4. What else did you succeed in today?

   _____

   _____

5. What can you do better tomorrow?

   _____

   _____

6. What is something for which you are grateful today?

   _____

   _____

7. Progress Notes:

   _____

   _____

   _____

Day 4 - Figuring Out Your Deeper Needs

"We are driven by five genetic needs: survival, love and belonging, power, freedom, and fun." — William Glasser

"It seems to me we can never give up longing and wishing while we are thoroughly alive. There are certain things we feel to be beautiful and good, and we must hunger after them." — George Eliot

"Men make counterfeit money; in many more cases, money makes counterfeit men." — Sydney J. Harris

If urges have one benefit, it's that they're really, really good at highlighting our unconscious needs.

If you're married or have kids, you may be familiar with pregnancy food cravings. During pregnancy, a woman can develop intense cravings for unusual foods and even non-food items! The science behind pregnancy cravings says that it's the body's way of searching for specific nutrients necessary for the development of the fetus. Even craving unhealthy foods such as chocolate cake may indicate specific nutrient deficiencies such as vitamin K, iron, and folate which happen to be high in chocolate cake!

Sexual urges often work in the same way in that they indicate we have unmet needs. Instead of gorging on "chocolate cake" or PMO, try to identify the *deeper* need behind it. Find the need, and you can replace it with a healthier alternative.

Now, many people call "sex" the need itself. I disagree. There are two primary sources of sexual urges. The first one is a deep love and desire to be intimate with someone you love and care for. If you have never experienced this, it's a feeling of deep love for the soul of that person, far above simply wanting them. The next trigger of sexual urges relates to brokenness. This is where most casual sexual urges originate. Perhaps you're chasing a rush or validation, or it may be you are running from something like stress or guilt.

Whenever you experience urges, try to identify your deeper need using the chart below.

Need / Want (Chasing)	Escape (Running From)	Healthy Solutions
Affirmation, validation, or recognition	Insecurity	Cultivate self-confidence & sexual wholeness; be what you need; love yourself
Reassurance, security	Fears	Self-assurance
Happiness, healing	Pain	Cultivate a feeling of "wholeness" by focusing on the present moment
Control	Lack of control	Cultivate a strong feeling of personal control and opportunity; establish a space of structure and routine
To let go, let loose	Too much responsibility	Cultivating a spontaneous or free space without decisions
Feelings, pleasure, high	Current physical experience	Contentment; experiencing the moment
Release	Hormones, urges	Experience them; learn to coexist with yourself; find meaning in them
Excitement	Boredom / Depression	Pursue balance, contentment, be okay with your natural cycles of highs and lows
Confidence, peace of mind	God, your conscience	Identify what needs to change and take ownership

Freedom, individuality, expression	Control, judgment	A place to express your interests and personality such as art or hobby
Rest, peace	Stress	Find balance; self-care; meditation; take a break
To be appreciated; enjoyed	Feeling useless or meaningless	Sexually validate yourself; appreciate yourself; search for deeper meaning and worth in your life beyond sexuality

Journaling:

Set aside some quiet time to explore your deeper needs. Ask yourself the following questions, and record your thoughts. It may take more than one session to come up with these. Come back to this section and add to it as you discover new needs

What do you crave most?

_____

_____

_____

_____

_____

What needs currently feel unmet?

_____

_____

_____

_____

_____

What drives (if not love) could be triggering your sexual urges?

_____

_____

_____

_____

_____

How can you satisfy urges in a healthy way?

_____

_____

_____

_____

_____

What changes can you make in your life/lifestyle to better fulfill your true needs?

_____

Affirmations:

- I am enough.
- I have enough.
- I don't need anyone else to validate me.
- I can meet my own emotional needs.

Daily Review

Streak Length: _____   **Days to Goal:** _____   **Did you succeed today?** _____

1. How would you rate your urges on a scale of 0-10? *(Give yourself a pat on the back if they were higher than normal and you still succeeded!)* _____

2. *How would you rate your mood on a scale of 0-10?* _____

3. How would you rate your energy on a scale of 0-10? _____

4. What else did you succeed in today?

   _____

   _____

5. What can you do better tomorrow?

   _____

   _____

6. What is something for which you are grateful today?

   _____

   _____

7. Progress Notes:

   _____

   _____

   _____

DAY 5 - ONE MORE DAY AT A TIME

"If you can quit for a day, you can quit for a lifetime." — Benjamin Sáenz

Clearly, it's easier to quit something for one day than it is to be perfect for 100 days, and it's easier to follow through with a one-day goal, than it is for a year. So why not complete 100 days by completing just **one day at a time?**

The reality is, **one day is never too much to ask from yourself. You can do anything for 24 hours.** Even when that voice in your head protests and says, *"I can't do this anymore. I can't get through today,"* I want you to respond with all the energy you can: *"Yes! I can. Just one... more... day."*

Whenever you lose sight of your new objective and who you want to become, old habits easily slip in and take over. Whether you struggle feeling like long-term recovery is too difficult, or wishing you could simply fast-forward to the end, breaking the challenge up into *"one day at a time"* is a sure-fire way to push through discouraging thoughts.

And here's the magic of taking it one day at a time. If you can do it one day, then why not 2 or 3? And if you can do it for 3 days, why not 6? And if you can do it 6 whole days, then you can certainly manage another one to make it to 7! **It is just *one* day.** You *can and will* get through it.

So rather than worrying in terms of months or years ahead, just focus your attention on today. Today is what matters. "Baby steps," remember?

Affirmations:

- I can get through today.
- It is just one day. I will focus on staying clean today.
- I am proud of myself for reaching day 5.

Daily Review

Streak Length: _____   **Days to Goal:** _____   **Did you succeed today?** _____

1. How would you rate your urges on a scale of 0-10? *(Give yourself a pat on the back if they were higher than normal and you still succeeded!)* _____

2. How would you rate your mood on a scale of 0-10? _____

3. How would you rate your energy on a scale of 0-10? _____ ;

4. What else did you succeed in today?
   _____
   _____

5. What can you do better tomorrow?
   _____
   _____

6. What is something for which you are grateful today?
   _____
   _____

7. Progress Notes:
   _____
   _____
   _____

Day 6 - Recurring Negative Thoughts

If you are still in the fight, **CONGRATULATIONS**! You are entering one of the hardest parts of this fight. Stay vigilant, and don't give up. Things will get easier soon, but you must keep pushing through those urges!

"The happiness of your life depends upon the quality of your thoughts: therefore, guard accordingly, and take care that you entertain no notions unsuitable to virtue and reasonable nature." — Marcus Aurelius

"It is the mark of an educated mind to be able to entertain a thought without accepting it." — Aristotle

"A silly idea is current that good people do not know what temptation means. This is an obvious lie. Only those who try to resist temptation know how strong it is... A man who gives in to temptation after five minutes simply does not know what it would have been like an hour later. That is why bad people, in one sense, know very little about badness. They have lived a sheltered life by always giving in." — C. S. Lewis

"The battles that count aren't the ones for gold medals. The struggles within yourself - the invisible, inevitable battles inside all of us - that's where it's at." — Jesse Owens

Your Thoughts Matter

Learning to drive at the age of 16, I was given the simple advice, *"Always look where you want the car to go."* By keeping your eyes fixed on the center of the lane ahead, you're able to maintain a smooth course. However, looking off to the side of the road, will cause the vehicle to veer in that direction. This is why drunk drivers so often crash into landmarks and people — they inadvertently drive towards whatever they're looking at!

This phenomenon is called 'target fixation,' and it happens when a person "becomes so focused on an observed object (be it a target or hazard) that they inadvertently increase their risk of colliding with the object." (Wikipedia)

Target fixation is not just a phenomenon on the road, though. It occurs constantly in our *minds*. Whatever we *think* about ultimately determines the direction we go in *life*.

You are no doubt familiar with the expressions, "you are what you eat" and "you are what you think." If you are constantly *thinking* about porn, shame, doubt, or failure you will unconsciously increase your risk of making those thoughts a *reality*.

Here's an example. I once worked with someone who was constantly thinking, talking, and posting about how much he *hated* the porn industry. Although he was thinking about how toxic the industry is and how it had negatively impacted him, those thoughts ultimately led him into relapse after relapse in a vicious cycle.

Alternatively, by focusing on **sobriety, goals, a 'better version of *you*,' and success**, you will increase your risk of "colliding" with them. And wouldn't that be a *shame* — to increase your risk of **success** and **growth**?! (Kidding of course). That's the goal, and that's why <u>learning to manage your thoughts is critical to your success!</u>

Coping With Recurring Negative Thoughts

Cast your mind back to science class at school for a moment. Newton's Second Law of Thermodynamics says: "Without added input, everything moves towards entropy, chaos, and deterioration." At least, that's my hazy recollection of it. The point is not the specifics of thermodynamics, though, it's the natural law of entropy. Without positive input, everything including our thoughts, tend to spiral out of control. As humans, we all suffer recurring negative thoughts of some sort whether they're insecurities, fears, temptations, frustrations, and so on. It happens to everyone.

"Recurring negative thoughts" are the unwanted thoughts of insecurity, fear, frustrations, fantasies, or memories that plague us all. They are the thoughts that seem to be there even though we don't want them, and they keep coming back.

To prevent and recover from these negative mental cycles, we must learn to *replace* these negative thoughts with more positive, helpful, and motivating ones, and do that consistently.

Here's how to understand and correct negative thoughts.

#1: The first step is identifying the source of these thoughts. Is it a specific trigger? Is it a pattern of thought? What came *before* the negative thought? Use the chart below or write in your journal.

<u>Example</u>
Negative Thought: "I'm no good."
Trigger: A thought of a failed relationship.

Negative thought: _____

_____

Trigger/ trigger thought: _____

_____

Negative thought: _____

_____

Trigger/ trigger thought: _____

_____

#2: The next step is to actively choose better thoughts. Remember the Second Law of Thermodynamics we discussed? If you are not consciously choosing positivity, your brain will always slip into the negative. For you to be successful, it's important that you learn to dismiss negative thoughts and replace them with positive, motivating ones.

Example: Negative thought: "I'll never be able to quit." Positive counter thought: "People quit every day; the choice is mine. I will stay in the fight and make it happen."

Example: Negative thought: "Just one more time, relapse won't hurt." Positive counter thought: "Staying clean will improve my confidence, my health, my relationships, and my goals."

Negative thought: _____

_____

Positive Counter thought: _____

_____

Negative thought: _____

_____

Positive Counter thought: _____

_____

What are a few examples of negative thoughts you experience, and what do you believe are the triggers and sources?

_____

_____

Why is it important to create a healthy ecosystem in your mind? What does a healthy relationship with yourself look like?

Affirmations:

After completing the exercises above, continue exploring key affirmations that will help you to reach your goals. What positive self-talk will motivate you this week? (What would you want to hear from a friend?)

Daily Review

Streak Length: _____ **Days to Goal:** _____ **Did you succeed today?** _____

1. How would you rate your urges on a scale of 0-10? *(Give yourself a pat on the back if they were higher than normal and you still succeeded!)* _____

2. How would you rate your mood on a scale of 0-10? _____

3. How would you rate your energy on a scale of 0-10? _____

4. What else did you succeed in today?

   _____

   _____

5. What can you do better tomorrow?

   _____

   _____

6. What is something for which you are grateful today?

   _____

   _____

7. Progress Notes:

   _____

   _____

   _____

Day 7 - Using Your Sexual Energy for Success

"The generative energy, which, when we are loose, dissipates and ... when we are continent invigorates and inspires us. Chastity is the flowering of man; and what are called Genius, Heroism, Holiness, and the like, are but various fruits which succeed it." — Henry *David Thoreau*

"By having sex, you waste a lot of energy. I mean, the vital energy in your body goes away... but if you want to accumulate energy, if you want to get full energy, you cannot waste." — Rickson Gracie, MMA, and Jiu-Jitshu Legend

"Our birth control method up to that point was Steve's coitus interruptus, also called the pull-out method, which for him was about his conserving his energy for work,' she wrote. He explained that he didn't want to climax so he could build 'power and wealth by conserving one's vital energies.'" — Chrisann Brennan, referring to her relationship with Steve Jobs

Today is all about using your peak testosterone in a positive way. On average, 7 days after ejaculation men have 40% more testosterone! Therefore, it's likely that your urges are still at an all-time high today. *Sexual transmutation* is the idea of using your sexual energy to inspire and strengthen you. Your mission today is to use that energy to reach a new goal or tackle a project.

When you experience high-energy urges, it's best to use them in an active, physical way: sports, hiking, a workout, etc. If unwanted sexual thoughts are overwhelming, you can try a mind clearing meditation (as on Day 3) or focus on staying distracted. Another distraction that may help you is to watch practical or motivational videos that relate to something you are working on or are passionate about. Doing so may help you get the focus to stay clean.

Meditation:

Set a 10-minute timer. Your goal is to find inner peace. Peace exists within your body. It's accessible when you search for it. But first, you may have to make a conscious decision to accept yourself. Practice acceptance, be proud of yourself, and find that inner peace.

Affirmations:

Repeat the affirmations you wrote down yesterday in addition to the following:

- I am strong.
- I am powerful.
- I am focused on my goals.
- My urges do not control me.

DAILY REVIEW

Streak Length: _____ **Days to Goal:** _____ **Did you succeed today?** _____

1. How would you rate your urges on a scale of 0-10? *(Give yourself a pat on the back if they were higher than normal and you still succeeded!)* _____

2. How would you rate your mood on a scale of 0-10? _____

3. How would you rate your energy on a scale of 0-10? _____

4. What else did you succeed in today?

   _____

   _____

5. What can you do better tomorrow?

   _____

   _____

6. What is something for which you are grateful today?

   _____

   _____

7. Progress Notes:

   _____

   _____

   _____

Day 8 - Time to Celebrate!

"Many of life's failures are people who did not realize how close they were to success when they gave up." — Thomas Edison

"If there is no struggle, there is no progress." — Frederick Douglass

Congratulations! Today is a big day and it's time to celebrate. Successfully completing your first week on this journey is a big achievement, and you should be proud of yourself. You deserve a day of celebration, so consider this a friendly reminder to do something nice for yourself!

Journaling:

What benefits have you noticed so far in your journey?

_____

_____

_____

Affirmations:

- I am on this journey for myself.
- It matters to me.
- I deserve success.
- I will push forward & stay away from porn because my future is worth it.

Daily Review

Streak Length: _____   **Days to Goal:** _____   **Did you succeed today?** _____

1. How would you rate your urges on a scale of 0-10? *(Give yourself a pat on the back if they were higher than normal and you still succeeded!)* _____

2. How would you rate your mood on a scale of 0-10? _____

3. How would you rate your energy on a scale of 0-10? _____

4. What else did you succeed in today?

   _____

   _____

5. What can you do better tomorrow?

   _____

   _____

6. What is something for which you are grateful today?

   _____

   _____

7. Progress Notes:

   _____

   _____

   _____

Section 4

Reaching 30 Days & Beyond

The Next Steps in Your Journey

Did you make it your first week yet? If not, that's okay! We have 24 more strategies to help rewire your brain and achieve full recovery!

This section is for you to "go at your own pace." Work through lessons as needed, and feel free to skip forward to lessons that apply to you and your needs in recovery. Only "Day 15" and "Day 30 Clean" (the day you reach a full 30 days of abstinence!) should be done in time with your abstinence streak since these checkpoints are meant to celebrate these key benchmarks in your journey.

Since this section is more flexible, you will find additional *Daily Review* pages in the back for continued daily tracking!

Strategies you will find in this section:

- 9. Keeping Sexuality in Proper Perspective
- 10. Life IS a Challenge
- 11. The Dangers of Lust
- 12. Real Love
- 13. Beasts & Dragons: There is No Immunity
- 14. Forgiveness
- **Day 15 Clean:** Review
- 16. Balancing The Past, Present, and Future
- 17. Defining Yourself: Who are you?
- 18. Ego: The Enemy Within
- 19. Confidence & Attractiveness
- 20. Humility & Modesty
- 21. Leaving Your Comfort Zone
- 22. Loneliness
- 23. Discovering Your Values
- 24. What Sex Is, Isn't, & should be
- 25. Making Amends
- 26. The Purpose of Doubt
- 27. Habits & Muscle Memory
- 28. Gratitude
- 29. Natural Law
- 30. Pride vs. Healthy Self-Esteem
- **Day 30 Clean.** Do you want to continue?

9. Keeping Sexuality in Proper Perspective

"Sexual thoughts, temptations, attractions, are part of being human, but it's how you respond to them. We don't do things or engage ourselves in things where sexual gratification will be the end." — Rev. Shawn McKnight.

"Sex is a need... to the continuation of the life of the species; not that of the animal, or the person." — Mokokoma Mokhonoana

"Celibacy is not just a matter of not having sex. It is a way of admiring a person for their humanity, maybe even for their beauty." — Timothy Radcliffe

Why are sexual addictions so hard to quit? And why do they affect us so deeply? You may be worried or wondering if your recovery means never experiencing sex or orgasm again, and that's an understandable concern.

The most important thing to remember is that although your sexuality is an integral part of who you are, it does not *define* you. There is *so* much more to life, and it's important to keep sexuality in proper perspective.

Whether you are married, dating, or single, if your sexuality has taken the front seat in your life, it's time to restructure and re-prioritize. Things have become out of balance!

Compare the following statements to your own life, to determine if sex has dominated your life in an unhealthy way:

1. You are often distracted by sexual thoughts while doing other things.

2. You've allowed your sexual desires to take precedence over more important goals (spirituality, relationships, work, etc.).

3. You spend more time watching porn or masturbating than you do on self-development.

4. You get frustrated with your partner when he or she does not satisfy your urges on *your* time, or in a specific way you want.

5. You neglect important obligations and give priority to selfish sexual satisfaction.

6. Porn, masturbation, and having sex cause you to be late for appointments, work, or other serious responsibilities.

Journaling:

If any of the above symptoms describe or resonate with you, the following journal exercise will help you start to restructure sexuality's role in your life:

What is your mission in life?

_____

_____

_____

_____

_____

_____

How much thought or time do you waste on sex?

_____

_____

_____

_____

_____

What benefits are there in taking a break from sex (temporary or permanent)?

_____

_____

_____

_____

_____

_____

What aspects of your life have been neglected by the overemphasis of sex?

_____

_____

_____

_____

_____

_____

How can taking a "break from sexuality" boost your personal development?

_____

_____

_____

_____

_____

_____

_____

Navigating The Goodbye

In many ways, quitting an addiction is like a toxic break up. To be fair, recovery means giving up something that you believe you like, enjoy, or otherwise benefit from — and that's not easy! It's an emotional struggle and a sacrifice that may produce feelings of grief, or a fear of moving on.

Sometimes we *must* move on from things we 'love,' for our own growth and happiness, and it's okay to grieve while choosing to move forward. It's a part of life.

As you work through your feelings of grief and fear, it's okay to practice acceptance and honesty about what you are letting go, while prioritizing the benefits of recovery.

It's a hard decision, but remember, this is for a positive purpose, and it will unquestionably be worth it in the long run!

Affirmations:

- Sex is not a *need*.
- I am more than sexuality.
- This will all be worth it.
- I am not giving up my sexuality, rather I am taking a break from its use.

10. LIFE *IS* A CHALLENGE

"The game of life is a lot like football. You have to tackle your problems, block your fears, and score your points when you get the opportunity." — Lewis Grizzard

"Those who approach life like a child playing a game, moving and pushing pieces, possess the power of kings." — Heraclitus

"Do you think any man can find true happiness elsewhere than his natural state; and when you try to spare him all suffering, are you not taking him out of his natural state?" — Jean-Jacques Rousseau

"If you would only recognize that life is hard, things would be so much easier for you." — Louis D. Brandeis

Think back, for a moment, to a time you were stuck on a difficult game or puzzle, one you just couldn't beat. What did you do when confronted with the challenge? Were you determined to defeat it? Did you stay up late trying to figure it out? Or perhaps you can think of a skill you tried to master, failing countless times before finally claiming victory?

When it comes to games and hobbies, we often *enjoy* the challenge. But in life, not so much. The "Game of Life" also presents us with a series of challenges. However, instead of accepting challenges with determination and pleasure, we tend to treat them as *inconveniences* and *disasters*.

At one time or another we have all asked the questions: Why me? Why is this so hard? Why do I have to experience this? We instinctively prefer peace, tranquility, and bliss, and yet we consistently experience pain, discomfort, and challenges. It's not anyone's fault. It's simply the way nature works. The good news is that your journey can also be heroic. **It all depends on how you choose to view your experiences.** By accepting and appreciating the *challenges* of life — we can find deeper contentment and even joy in the journey.

To do this requires a significant change in perspective, one that embraces nature for what it is and isn't. Consider the following perspective changes, which are crucial to finding inner peace:

1. **You must understand that the present moment *is not the end*.** It is only a scene, or a chapter, in your story. The present moment is fleeting, and nothing ever stays the same.

2. **Our existence on Earth will never be "*perfect*" in a Utopian sense.** That simply does not exist on Earth. The natural state of our existence here is chaos, death, and deterioration. However, happiness and enlightenment can be found in embracing this reality and accepting nature.

3. **Life will continuously present new challenges.** That is simply a given. How you face those challenges, however, determines your growth. *Are you progressing or simply pushing through?*

Life is a challenge meant to be won. *Embrace it. Thrive on it. Grow from it. This is your opportunity, privilege, and blessing.*

I love this message from the *Discourse of Epictetus*:

"What would have become of Hercules do you think if there had been no lion, hydra, stag or boar — and no savage criminals to rid the world of? What would he have done in the absence of such challenges? Obviously, he would have just rolled over in bed and gone back to sleep. So, by snoring his life away in luxury and comfort, he never would have developed into the mighty Hercules. And even if he had, what good would it have done him? What would have been the use of those arms, that physique, and that noble soul, without crises or conditions to stir into him action?"

Do you view the challenges and trials of life as an opportunity for growth and heroism? Or as an inconvenience? **Choose wisely.** It will determine your destiny!

Journaling:

Write down a list of past challenges you can recall and the lessons you learned from each one.

_____

_____

_____

_____

_____

How did you grow?

_____

_____

_____

_____

_____

How did it shape your character or knowledge?

_____

_____

_____

_____

What important lessons might you not have learned had you not had those challenges?

___

___

___

___

___

___

___

Kobe Bryant said, "Everything negative - pressure, challenges - is all an opportunity for me to rise." How can you RISE from your present challenges?

___

___

___

___

___

Meditation and Journaling:

Spend some time on this chapter, digesting it carefully. Then, record your thoughts below.

Try visualizing your life as a game. What level are you on? What challenges do you face? How will you overcome them? What will it take to progress to the next level? What positives can you find in the current moment? What good things are happening right now?

_____

_____

_____

_____

_____

_____

_____

_____

_____

_____

_____

Affirmations:

- Life is a game.
- I can do this.
- This is a challenge/situation I'm meant to figure out.
- Today's challenges are an opportunity for growth.
- I will find solutions

11. THE DANGERS OF LUST

"Imagination is all too often wasted on masturbation." — Mokokoma Mokhonoana

"I think lust is a very different thing from love. I believe in sex love." — Mahatma Gandhi

"The way to chastity is not to struggle with incontinent thoughts but to avert the thoughts by some employment, or by reading, or by meditating on other things." — Sir Isaac Newton in a letter to John Locke

I was walking through a grocery store when a woman wearing obnoxiously revealing clothing stepped in front of me. Suddenly, I realized she had been the first woman I'd noticed the entire time I'd been in the store.

Interestingly, however, I noticed plenty of men, including those who were wearing wedding rings and those who were not. It's not that I was thinking any sexual thoughts, but I was clearly noticing men and paying no attention to the women. Although this is largely instinctual, it's completely possible to retrain your brain on what you want to notice and what you don't. The first step is realizing you're doing it, and the next is to commit to stop.

Lust is at the core of sex-based addictions. Not only is it a key trigger, but overcoming it is an essential part of your long-term healing. Lust is typically defined as a feeling of longing or "wanting someone," particularly in a sexual way. Although there can be many applications of the word "lust", for this book, we will focus solely on the sexual definition of lust or *wanting someone sexually*.

With raging hormones, living in a hyper-sexualized world, it can be very difficult to manage thoughts. Left untamed, though, lustful thoughts can destroy you from the inside out. It starts in your head but soon you feel a burning in your chest, arousal in your sexual organs, your breathing becomes faster, and so on. This unsatisfying, partial arousal can then lead to all sorts of frustration, insecurity, anger, resentment, and even self-hate.

Fighting and conquering the 'beast' of lust is a serious battle of the heart that requires self-discipline, but it's one that's well worth fighting. It will change you at your very core, for the better, giving you more mental clarity and deeper spirituality. It will also heal your relationship with God, and even restore feelings of empathy and natural love that may have been lost along the way.

Journaling:

Where does your lust come from? A feeling of emptiness? A hunger? The impulse to conquer? Or perhaps rebelliousness? Ponder this question, and write down your thoughts:

_____

_____

_____

_____

_____

What does lust feel like? What do you get out of it? Dig deep and figure out why you take that second look, or fall into inappropriate thoughts?

_____

_____

_____

_____

_____

What beliefs do you have about lust? Do you believe it is normal and healthy, or can you see the dangers? What social influences have shaped your beliefs? What do you believe personally now that you're expanding your knowledge and understanding?

_____

_____

_____

_____

Is lust something you allow, or is it something that 'happens to you'?

_____

_____

_____

_____

Another great way to deal with lust is to focus on a person's inner *qualities* versus their *appearance*. What character qualities do you value in others?

_____

_____

_____

_____

_____

If you're a single person and you're looking for a potential partner, what qualities matter most to you? And what can you do to find a person with those qualities?

_____
_____
_____
_____
_____

What do you value in others?

_____
_____
_____
_____
_____

What does respect mean to you?

_____
_____
_____
_____
_____

12. REAL LOVE

"With Real Love, nothing else matters; without it, nothing else is enough." — Greg Baer

"In real love you want the other person's good. In romantic love you want the other person." — Margaret Anderson

"True charity is the desire to be useful to others with no thought of recompense." — Emanuel Swedenborg

We are in a confusing time where love has become fractured. Many people are selfish, families are falling apart, couples are separating after 20+ years of marriage, and many people don't feel loved.

What is the meaning of "love"? While the word is sometimes used in a sexual context, fundamentally the word describes a wide variety of situations that involve connection, such as the tender feelings of a mother and her newborn, or the sacrifices of a solider for his comrades. Interestingly, this wide variety of meanings of the word love is nicely reflected in the Greek language, where they have four distinct words for love: eros, philia, storge, and agape.

Real love though, in its purest, deepest form, is *charity*. And what is charity?

"Charity is more than love, far more; it is everlasting love, perfect love.... It is love so centered in righteousness that the possessor has no aim or desire except for the eternal welfare of his own soul and for the souls of those around him." — Bruce R. McConkie

In other words, *real love* is perfectly selfless, kind, patient, and enduring. *Real love* cares about the heart and soul of the other person. It is not about what you can selfishly *get* from a relationship, but rather about what you can *give*. Charity doesn't feel the need to criticize, control, or prove a point, but rather inspire, uplift, and serve.

It's been said, "porn kills love," and I've certainly observed that to be true. Not only does it damage your ability to *feel* loved, but it limits your ability to love others. Lust, the objectification of others, and the unnatural practice of sex without intimacy, damages one's ability to empathize and connect deeply with everyone around.

Without real love, relationships and hearts suffer. The good news, however, is that this negative effect of porn **can** be reversed and healed! I've witnessed time and time again the powerful effect that recovery has on one's capacity for *real love*. It is one of the greatest benefits of recovery! Through the intentional practice of genuine kindness, you can heal the wounds of addiction, and in turn, the healing process will open up a greater capacity for real love. It's a win/win!

Meditation:

What does real love feel like?

_____

_____

_____

_____

When have you experienced it? Can you think of a person or a place where you felt real love?

_____

_____

_____

_____

What is real love? Where does it come from? And how do you develop it?

If you have a religious inclination, what do the scriptures say about the word "charity"? How can you develop 'charity'?

What is the difference between real love and selfish or addictive love?

_____

_____

_____

_____

What are some things you do or can do to show real love for those around you?

_____

_____

_____

_____

Affirmations:

- I am worthy of love.
- Real love exists.
- I will embody the love I desire to receive.

Additional Resources About Real Love and Addiction:

- "Real Love" by Greg Baer
- "The Power of Now" or "Practicing The Power of Now" by Eckhart Tolle
- "Heart of Man" - 2019 film directed by Eric Esau

13. BEASTS & DRAGONS: THERE IS NO IMMUNITY

"If you know the enemy and know yourself you need not fear the results of a hundred battles." — Sun Tzu

"Whoever fights monsters should see to it that in the process he does not become a monster. And if you gaze long enough into an abyss, the abyss will gaze back into you." — Friedrich Nietzsche

The bottom line is that some beasts are too strong to fight alone, and some beasts you must avoid altogether. Knowing your limitations is not a weakness. It is wisdom. Pornography and sexual addiction is the enemy.

It is a false notion to think that recovery is developing an *immunity* to the beast when in reality, *victory* is all about developing a new mindset to *resist* its solicitations altogether. To not give in because it no longer appeals to you.

You may have heard the phrase, *"Once an addict always an addict."* I don't agree with that. You are no longer an addict whenever you choose to quit and flee from the beast, but should you hesitate, look back, or give in, it awakens again within you. To defeat addiction, it must be starved. In giving the beast even an inch, it grows, and should you slip, it may devour you.

When it comes to addiction, there is no immunity, only total abstinence.

There's an old Western pioneer story that goes something like this: A man was interviewing wagon drivers for a very important position of transporting gold. Each of the applicants would boast about how close they could get to the edge of the canyon or cliff while maintaining control of the wagon and horses. One would say, "I can ride within a foot." Another would say, "I can ride within 2 inches."

Then a man came in explaining that he would always choose the *safest* route and remain as *far* from the edge as possible.

Which driver do you think was hired for the job? Who would **you** hire to transport such a valuable cargo?

Pornography is a poison that will hurt you in even the smallest doses. It is a distraction and pollution, and the only way to truly overcome it is to avoid it in every possible way. Would you eat a meal poisoned with only a *little bit* of arsenic? Of course not! In the same way, you cannot expect to consume a *little bit* of pornography and not be negatively affected.

When it comes to pornography, there is no "maintaining control" or "safely riding the edge". Getting close to the beast *in any capacity* (peeking, softcore porn, etc.) is still failing. In this kind of flirting with the edge, you're putting yourself and others at risk and getting distracted from your mission — essentially losing to the beast.

Your objective setting out was living a porn-free life! Remember that, and stay focused. You can do it.

Affirmations:

- Addiction is a beast I can and will conquer.
- I have the strength within me to improve my life.
- I will not give in.
- I have the power to choose recovery.

14. FORGIVENESS

"To forgive is to set a prisoner free and discover that the prisoner was you." — Lewis B. Smedes

"To err is human; to forgive, divine." — Alexander Pope

"You can survive tough situations and even turn them to your advantage by acting as if you are the person you want to be. When you act like that person, you can become that person. The hard parts are deciding whom you want to become, being willing to rehearse until you become that person, and forgiving yourself until you do." — Bernie Siegel

When you think of forgiveness, who do you think of first? Those who have wronged you? Or perhaps someone you've hurt?

Do you think of God and the forgiveness you seek? What about yourself? It's said that addiction is the only prison with the locks on the inside. Carrying the heavy chains of guilt, shame, regret, and self-hatred can make recovery an impossible journey. That's why forgiveness is the key.

One of the biggest hurdles in the addiction recovery process is overcoming the negative thoughts and memories of our past. By this point, you've likely been worn down with the burden of knowing how many people you've hurt or let down, including yourself. You may feel that your mistakes are too great or that your past is too dark. You may also feel that you don't deserve forgiveness.

Admittedly, our own self is often the hardest person to forgive, but the process is very similar to the coming section on "Making Amends." After you have apologized to those who you have wronged, it's time to forgive yourself. You will then be able to unlock the prison door and step into the light. Remember, what counts is not what's in the past, but it's what you do now!

Here are the key components of an apology as steps for forgiving yourself:

1. Acknowledge responsibility and take full ownership.
2. Allow yourself to feel regret and sincere remorse.
3. Identify what went wrong.
4. Allow yourself to accept God's grace.
5. Choose forgiveness. Say *"I am going to forgive myself for…."*
6. Make the necessary changes and/or establish a plan to.
7. Let it go.

Journaling:

To aid your full recovery, it's vital to put the past behind you and stop dwelling on it. Review the following questions to help you overcome your regrets:

What knowledge, skills, or tools did you lack then that you have now?

_____

_____

_____

_____

_____

How have you grown from the mistakes?

_____

_____

_____

_____

_____

_____

_____

What positive outcomes came from the mistake? (Try to find at least ONE positive outcome.)

_____

_____

_____

_____

_____

What makes you worthy of forgiveness?

_____

_____

_____

_____

_____

How will forgiveness improve your life and set you free?

_____

_____

_____

_____

_____

Other Tips for Self-Forgiveness Include:

- Set a date to "let it go"
- Have a small ceremony or letter burning
- Meditate
- Write yourself an "I forgive you" letter

Affirmations:

- I will treat myself with respect and kindness from today forward.
- I have greatly improved my knowledge and understanding
- I have the courage to heal
- The past no longer exists.
- I learned from my mistake and will keep moving forward.

DAY 15. REVIEW YOUR PROGRESS, REASON, & PLAN

Journaling:

How do you feel overall about your journey so far?

_____

_____

_____

_____

What successful changes have you made?

_____

_____

_____

_____

What benefits have you seen or felt?

_____

_____

_____

_____

How has your life improved?

_____

_____

_____

_____

What additional changes would you like to achieve or what additional benefits would you like to see?

_____

_____

_____

_____

What steps can you take to get more out of this journey and achieve your goals?

_____

_____

_____

_____

What challenges have you encountered?

_____

_____

_____

_____

_____

What steps could you take to work through or alleviate these challenges?

_____

_____

_____

_____

What are the benefits of pressing forward?

_____

_____

_____

_____

Revisit Your Reason:

From Alice In Wonderland by Lewis Carroll:

> *Alice: "Would you tell me, please, which way I ought to go from here?"*
> *The Cheshire Cat: "That depends a good deal on where you want to get to."*
> *Alice: "I don't much care where."*
> *The Cheshire Cat: "Then it doesn't matter which way you go."*

Having clear direction and purpose is key to your success. It's good to periodically reassess your direction and reasons though. Growth, progress, time, and other factors may cause a shift that either weakens or changes your commitments. Staying focused and deliberate is important.

So, today, revisit your original reasons and commitments, and ask yourself the following questions.

Journaling:

Over the last few weeks, have my reasons changed or stayed the same?

_____

_____

_____

Has my vision for what I want to accomplish changed?

_____

_____

_____

_____

What key motivators will help me accomplish my goals?

_____

_____

_____

_____

Where do my core values and goals intersect, and how do they work together?

_____

_____

_____

Meditation:

Spend 10+ minutes meditating on your **motivating reasons.** Why do they still matter to you now and for your future? Record any additional thoughts:

_____

_____

_____

Affirmations:

- I can accomplish my goals.
- I can be who I want to be.
- I am doing my best, and that's what matters.
- I am proud of my progress so far.

Revisit Your Plan

"It was character that got us out of bed, commitment that moved us into action, and discipline that enabled us to follow through." — Zig Ziglar

"There are no secrets to success. It is the result of preparation, hard work, and learning from failure." — Colin Powell

How are you doing in following through with the list below?

- Using your exit strategy
- Following through on goals and revaluation dates
- Taking care of yourself in a healthy way
- Using distraction activities
- Seeking out real connection and socialization
- Communicating with your accountability/support person
- Removing or block triggers
- Setting aside a specific time for meditation and introspection each day
- Setting goals for other relevant lifestyle changes for your success

Honestly evaluate your success, failures, and habits for weaknesses and changes.

Affirmations:

- I do not need to be afraid of failure because I have a plan.
- I can achieve what I choose to achieve.
- I have the power.
- I am the only one who can make this choice for ME.

16. Balancing The Past, Present, and Future

Why Balance Is So Critical

While writing this book, I debated heavily on how, where, or *if* I should include this section at all. Although it doesn't seem directly related to porn or addiction recovery, *this may be* **the most important unit in the program.**

Anxiety, fear, regret, and fantasy are the main emotional causes of relapse. A well-adjusted sense of "presence" is the cure. Think of this lesson like a good chiropractic alignment. In proper balance and alignment, every aspect of your life functions better.

The decision to quit an addiction is the decision to become better and to be free. This begins with correcting your perceptions.

I love this quote by Eckhart Tolle: *"One could say that the only real problem is dysfunctional thinking, the rest are challenges, not problems."*

When it comes to dysfunctional thinking *(too much, too little, or completely flawed)*, the most common pitfalls are false perceptions of the past and future. For example, many people *fear the future* and *carry their past*s. These errors play major roles in our lives and addictions, so let's dissect them some more.

The Past

Traditional mental health therapy often focuses on "root causes" and traumas to find solutions for addiction problems. While I believe that such healing is a helpful part of the process, I disagree in calling it a *cause*. Let me explain…

The truth is, trauma was never the problem, only your perceptions of it. For instance, two people might experience the exact same circumstance and one develops terrible PTSD, while the other recovers and thrives. The difference lies in how they *processed* what happened, and what steps they took to overcome it.

Some of the traumas or past experiences frequently commonly cited as "causes for addiction" include:

- Abandonment
- Neglect
- Guilt
- Heart break
- Emotional abuse & bullying
- Sexual abuse
- Anger/resentment
- Broken relationships (typically with parents)
- Experiences of inferiority or failure
- Generational trauma /patterns
- And other experiences resulting in PTSD

Now, the most important thing to understand and accept is that *the past can't hurt you in the present, unless you allow it to.* That's because the past no longer exists — only your memory of it. The problem, and the pain, lies only in your choice to hold on to it.

You might think of the past like a bad splinter a child refuses to let be removed, keeping the child in unnecessary pain. The longer it stays in, the more it hurts, until it begins to swell, and possibly even become infected.

As mentioned before, we are all addicted to our own brokenness and pain, and *that* addiction is what keeps us entrenched in toxic behaviors. *But, remember:* **it's not hopeless — it's simply a process!**

The first step in healing and changing our perceptions is to **change the way we think about the past.** One of my favorite quotes is: *"The problem is the solution"* (Bill Mollison). Rather than seeing the past as a problem that prevented some more idealistic end, try to look for ways that your past **was** the solution, or in other words, provided resources for your future success. For example, a difficult childhood might help a person to mature more quickly, a painful breakup might reveal weaknesses or lead to a better opportunity, and so on.

Although holding onto painful, past experiences is by far the biggest issue we face with the past, there are other issues as well. A few of them include: making constant comparisons to the past, overthinking the past, missing the past, and daydreaming about the past can all get in the way of present goals and happiness. The past can be a great learning tool, but it's important to use it as such instead of letting it cause pain or become a distraction.

Journaling:

Now it's time to review your own life. Reflect and answer the following questions:

Establishing new perspectives of forgiveness, gratitude, and lessons learned are key ways to make progress. What lessons have you learned from your past experiences, and how can you use them to help you make improvements in the future?

_____

_____

_____

_____

What is an example of a "negative" experience from your past that has affected your life? Describe it below:

_____

_____

_____

_____

What emotions do you feel about that experience?

_____

_____

_____

_____

What problems did that experience solve (think: the problem was the solution)?

_____

_____

_____

_____

As you continue this journey of healing, try to identify other thought triggers that affect you throughout the day. For each memory or negative thought, you identify, explore, and write down answers to the following questions:

Which experiences do you find yourself holding onto, revisiting, or reliving?

_____

_____

_____

_____

What triggers (people, places, sights, sounds, etc.) send your mind there?

_____

_____

_____

_____

When do these thoughts usually occur (time of day, location, mood, etc.)?

_____

_____

_____

_____

How do those thoughts make you feel?

_____

_____

_____

_____

What problems did that past experience *solve* (think: the problem was the solution)? In other words, what was the benefit of going through that challenge?

_____

_____

_____

Is this something you want to frequently think about, or are you ready to let it go?

What additional steps could you take to heal and move on?

The Future

Now that we've addressed the past, it's time to look at the future. The future, like the past, does not actually exist. Rather it's an illusion, a concept. However, if your perceptions of it are unhealthy, it can trigger a wide array of mental, emotional, and physical problems that fuel addiction.

Even stress is a "future" problem — the fear that we may not have everything done on time or in the way we ideally want. Other "future" problems include fear of success, failure, change, losing control, and procrastination. Even loneliness tends to be a "future" problem stemming from thoughts and fears of being alone.

Fears are also an illusion that can trigger stress, and distract you from your capacity to achieve things right now, in the present. The fears of both success and failure can lead to indecision and inaction, and the fear of losing control distracts from your power and agency in the moment (which is effectively giving up control).

If you find yourself frequently caught up in the future, worrying about what might happen, there are two ways to redirect your mind: 1) focus on your *present* state and personal power, and 2) *visualize* the process of achieving success. Both of these strategies will help you move forward effectively, with courage and confidence.

Activity:

1. Refocus on the present:

MEDITATION Start by focusing on your physical sensations. How do you feel? What do you see or hear? What immediate circumstances do you need to handle? How will you act right now to deal with them?

2. Productive visualization:

Studies show that visualization can produce the same mental growth and some of the physical changes of an experience or action. This may be your most powerful tool regarding addiction recovery. To be addiction free, you must first conceptualize it and be able to see yourself achieving success. Mentally practicing resisting temptation and urges while in your "sober brain" will help prepare you mentally and physically for weaker moments.

VISUALIZATION Sit restfully and begin picturing your goals. What will it feel like to reach them? Can you see yourself accomplishing them? What steps will you take? Imagine successfully taking each one. Who will you be to get there?

Becoming & Being

Becoming

Because the past and future do not exist, all "problems" whether physical or mental, can only exist in the present. In the battle of addiction recovery, urges can be a very real challenge, causing overwhelming physical and mental distress. We will review some specific strategies for coping with the actual urges in a later chapter. Right now, we'll focus on the importance of *presence* and *being*.

Being

Now, remember: **"We cannot become, we can only choose to be."** Although "becoming" is a nice thought, in theory, it is still an illusion of the future with roots in the past. It's the idea that you "are not" and that something is preventing you from "being" (time, barriers, etc.).

Eckhart Tolle said it best: *"Nothing has happened in the past; it happened in the Now. Nothing will ever happen in the future; it will happen in the Now."* Even as the moments pass, you continually move with them. If you want to be someone different, *you can only be that person in the present moment.* If you want to achieve something, you can only choose to achieve it now, or at least choose to be on the journey.

As you shift your focus away from the illusions of the past and future and into the present, you must develop something with which you may have little experience, and that is your sense of being or your present state joined with your true potential.

I realize this is deep stuff. But it's important. To fight the beast, new tools and skills are needed, and this is one of them. If you're unsure about the meaning of this section, please go back and reread it again. It's vital to understand this important concept, especially if you are struggling to heal from past experiences.

Now, let's do something new. We're going to take your answers to the previous questions and shift them into the PRESENT. The goal is to shift your focus from the past and future to *being* in the moment — the only place where you can truly **be**.

Journaling:

What does sobriety feel like? (Spend a moment visualizing it right *now.*)

_____

_____

_____

_____

Who are you at this very moment? Do not include past or future. What defines you *now?*

_____

_____

_____

_____

Are you the person you want to be? Explain.

_____

_____

_____

_____

What can you be proud of right now?

_____

_____

_____

_____

What can you do to be the person you *want* to be right *now*?

_____

_____

_____

_____

Staying In The Present and Reality

As you shift your focus away from the illusions of the past and future and into the present, you must develop something you may have little experience with, and that is *your sense of being* or your present state joined with your true potential.

Stay Present

Staying in the present is actually the key to happiness. It means focusing on the here and now. Most problems exist in the past or the future. The present, however, has no grief and no fear. Without grief and fear, we'll find contentment and peace.

Oftentimes people try to escape reality and the present because it is too difficult or painful to be in, but when we leave reality and turn to fantasy, they only create more problems. Though we may experience difficulties in the present, they are not the same. They are simply challenges to overcome.

In addiction recovery, when struggling with urges or thoughts of relapse, staying in the present helps you to:

- Let go of past experiences that may be haunting, triggering, or bringing you down.
- Let go of the guilt and shame that keep you in relapse cycles.
- Un-imagine your fears of the future which may be discouraging you.
- Keep urges in perspective as a temporary challenge versus an indefinite and unbearable circumstance.

Sometimes staying present also means accepting a lower state or mood. As humans it's unrealistic to believe we can constantly be "over the moon." Our bodies and minds can't perpetually maintain a state of ecstasy, but that's okay. Everything in nature has highs, lows, ebbs, and flows. Instead of trying to run from your negative feelings with addiction, learn to explore them, and focus on finding peace and contentment in the now.

Meditation:

Practice being present by meditating on the following:

- Focusing on your senses is a great way to stay in or come back to the present. Close your eyes a moment. What do you feel in this moment?
- What do you have to be grateful for?
- Why is the present moment a *blessing*?
- Which challenges causing stress or pain for you are future or past related?
- Are there any real problems in *this moment*?

Stay in Reality

Another critical piece, similar to staying in the present, is staying in reality.

When we let our thoughts wander to either positive or negative fantasies, we leave the present. Though it may bring us pleasure in the moment to do that, dwelling on these thoughts only teases yourself, because they are in the end just fantasy.

So how exactly does fantasy differ from visualization, or namely the practice of visualizing success? The difference is that visualization, or manifestation, is a belief in what *can* exist, along with the purposeful, mindful, and strategic practice of attracting it. It is unquestionably a powerful tool for success. Fantasy, on the other hand, is a negative distraction and a waste of mental resources. Worse, it can lead to false expectations, disappointment, and even depression.

Remember, the present is all that truly exists, and it's the only place you can ever be truly happy. So rather than fantasizing on situations you *wish* would happen, try focusing on the reality of what you can actually *create* for yourself now. Consider the following quotes:

> "We are no longer happy so soon as we wish to be happier." -Walter Savage Landor

> "A conscious being whose powers were equal to his desires would be perfectly happy…. True happiness exists in decreasing the difference between our desires and our powers, in establishing a perfect equilibrium between the power [of achieving one's will] and the will." -Jean Jacques Rousseau

In order to be happy, our wants or desires ought to be within our ability to achieve them. In terms of sexual addiction, *wanting* someone or fantasizing about something you can't have, will only inevitably lead to more *unhappiness*. Fantasy only widens the gap between your desires and your ability to achieve them leaving you feeling hopeless or depressed.

Look, I'm well aware of the struggle. I'm human, just like you. When we're stressed out, our thoughts naturally wander off to places of fantasy for escape. We easily drift off into daydreams about pleasure, with no care in the world, but BAM! Whatever goes up, must come down, yes even our fantasies. When that happens, the fall can be crushing, and the return to reality can feel devastating, like waking up abruptly from a sweet dream you were really enjoying.

The bottom line is that whenever we escape to fantasy, *we always return grieving*. This applies to all vices commonly used to escape reality, including drugs and alcohol. The escape might feel good for a few moments, but you always have to return, with a rude awakening.

Is it not better then to embrace reality, conquer it, and mold it into the life you crave? Yes, you now have the exciting opportunity to design and create the most wonderful life!

Notes:

17. Defining Yourself: Who are you?

"Whatever we are, whatever we make of ourselves, is all we will ever have — and that, in its profound simplicity, is the meaning of life." — Philip Appleman

"Most of the shadows of this life are caused by standing in one's own sunshine." — Ralph Waldo Emerson

"It is not our mistakes that define who we are; it is how we recover from those mistakes." — Bo Bennett

The biggest difference between *Fight The Beast* and 12 step programs, is that we do not believe in defining yourself as an *addict*. You might be in recovery *from* an addiction, but YOU yourself are not an addict. You are an eternal being with incredible potential! The Beast — sexual addiction — does not *define* you. Rather, it is an antagonist in your story that you can and will conquer if you choose.

Today's lesson and activity is about defining your positive qualities. Who are you? What do you *like* about yourself? What gifts and talents do you have? It may be hard to acknowledge, but the fact is, you are a unique, special individual with many talents and abilities that others admire in you.

In the gingerbread man below, write some qualities you like about yourself. Continue doing this until you've filled in every empty space. You may only be able to think of a few at first, but the goal is to come up with 20-30+.

If you find this difficult, you might want to ask friends, co-workers, or family members what they admire about you.

1. _____

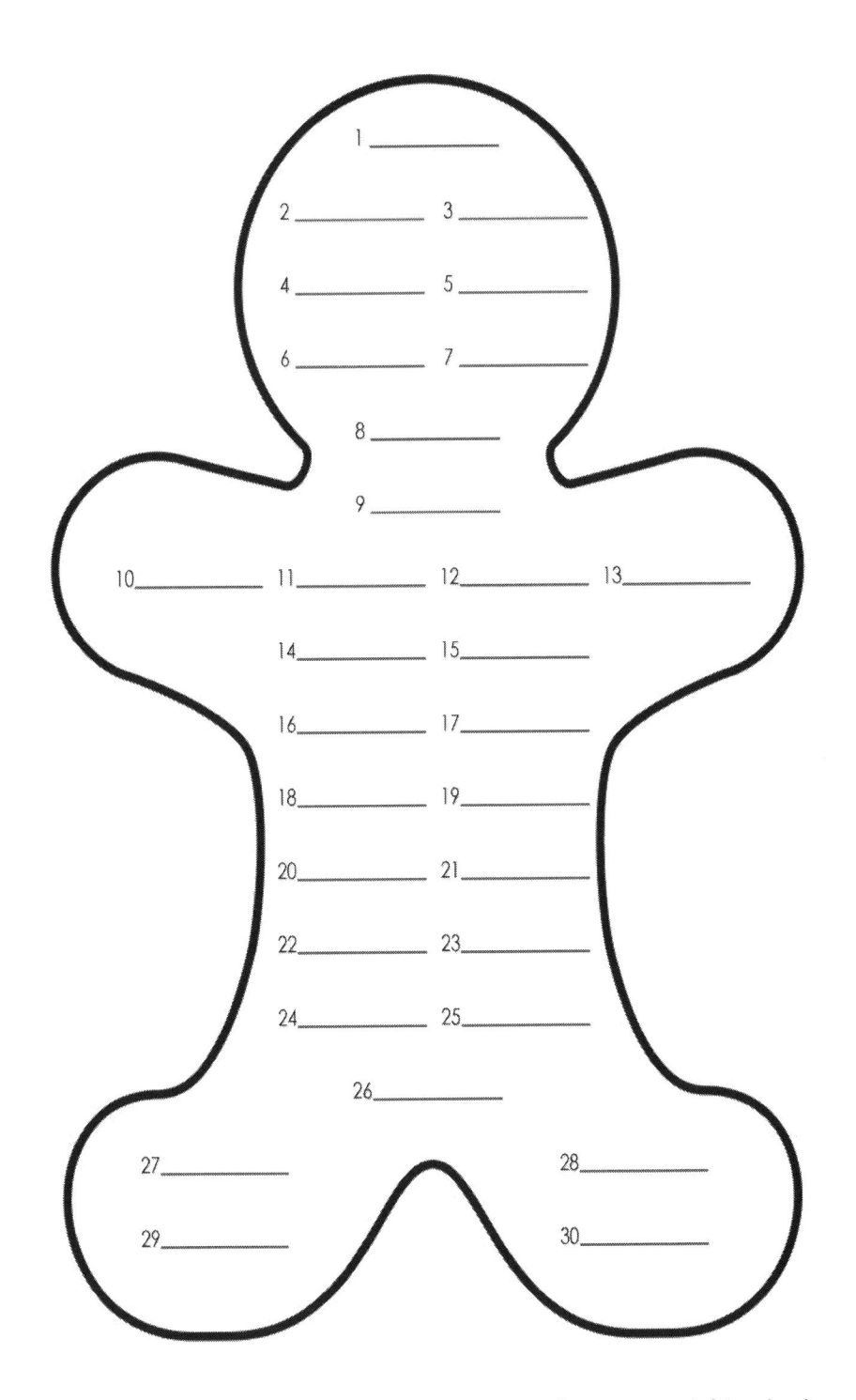

2. _____   3. _____

4. _____   5. _____

6. _____   7. _____

8. _____

9. _____

10. _____ 11. _____ 12. _____ 13. _____

14. _____   15. _____

16. _____   17. _____

18. _____   19. _____

20. _____   21. _____

22. _____   23. _____

24. _____   25. _____

26. _____

27. _____   28. _____

29. _____   30. _____

*Note: This Gingerbread man activity came from a good friend who specifically asked me to give credit to God for the inspiration He gave her, so I'm happy to acknowledge that here.

Affirmations:

Turn a few of the statements from the activity into affirmations, and say them out loud. I know this may feel uncomfortable to do, but all the more reason to do it! It *shouldn't* feel uncomfortable to appreciate yourself!

- "I am _____."
- "I am _____."
- "I am _____."
- "I am _____."
- "I am _____."
- "I am _____."
- "I am _____."
- "I am _____."
- "I am _____."
- "I am _____."

18. EGO: THE ENEMY WITHIN

"Addiction is the only prison where the locks are on the inside." — Unknown

"You can either be a host to God, or a hostage to your ego. It's your call." — Wayne Dyer

"Check your ego at the door. The ego can be the great success inhibitor. It can kill opportunities, and it can kill success." — Dwayne Johnson

Ego is at the core of many of life's problems, including addiction.

The ego is essentially the tangible, rigid way we define ourselves.

> *"The most common ego identifications have to do with possessions, the work you do, social status and recognition, knowledge and education, physical appearance, special abilities, relationships, personal and family history, belief systems, and other collective identifications. None of these is **you**."* — Eckhart Tolle

"You" are constantly changing, growing, progressing, and evolving. The ego, however, is contained and limited. It prevents us from positive change and growth by interfering with the process of identifying weaknesses in our lives and finding solutions. It prevents us from being honest with ourselves and others, as well as feeling a deep connection.

Our egos will stop at nothing to survive — including self-destruction. It tries to deceive you, reasoning: *"I'm okay as I am. I have everything under control. I've done nothing wrong, and all my problems are the fault of someone else."*

The ego resists anything that threatens our identity, whether positive or negative. In this mindset, we deny our weaknesses, resist growth, stay a victim, and develop animosity towards anyone or anything that might threaten or interfere with the identity our ego has established. Accepting responsibility for problems would be death to the ego identity. In some cases, the ego even resists positive change and growth in order to protect its past identities.

If you allow yourself to identify with your ego, it can keep you in a place of resistance, guilt, shame, and even addiction. If you think of yourself as an *addict* or an *alcoholic,* for instance, you're likely to stay that way. If you identify with unhealthy social or cultural trends you are also likely to remain trapped in that identity.

Eckhart Tolle explained, *"Complaining is one of the ego's favorite strategies for strengthening itself."* To survive, the ego projects blame for personal weaknesses and life's problems somewhere else. The ego feels it does not deserve problems, and it did not cause them. That's why it's so dangerous. It keeps you from seeing things as they truly are, and from taking ownership in your life.

Journaling:

What symptoms of ego's self-defense might come with your addiction?

_____
_____
_____
_____

What identities or beliefs might your ego be trying to defend or protect (whether positive or negative)?

_____
_____
_____
_____

Activity:

One way to get out of ego is to get out of your *head* and into *nature*.

Albert Einstein said, *"A human being is a part of the whole called by us 'universe'... He experiences himself, his thoughts and feelings as something separated from the rest, a kind of optical delusion of his consciousness. This delusion is a kind of prison for us, restricting us to our personal desires and to affection for a few persons nearest to us. Our task must be to free ourselves from this prison by widening our circle of compassion to embrace all living creatures and the whole of nature in its beauty."*

Try the following activity to connect with nature and dissolve the ego.

Take some time to sit in nature (a park, a garden, forest, etc.).

Pay attention to the life around you: the trees, animals, lichens, and insects. Notice how they all have a natural role and place. Notice the trees, how stable and confidently they stand, perfectly fulfilling their natural role. Spend some time quietly listening, then ask yourself the following:

What is my natural role?

_____

_____

_____

_____

What part do I have to play in this moment?

_____

_____

_____

What do I contribute to the universe?

Am I big or small compared to the world around me?

Do I obey the laws of nature, or am I out of alignment with my natural role?

What must I do to be in harmony with the world around me?

What am I meant to be in this moment and in the future?

19. CONFIDENCE & ATTRACTIVENESS

"Since love grows within you, so beauty grows. For love is the beauty of the soul." — Saint Augustine

In 2002, Dove, the popular soap and beauty brand, launched a marketing campaign with the message, "You're beautiful as you are, be confident in your skin!" It was an ad that changed the world, and it's even been called, "the greatest marketing campaign of the century." It was brilliant in terms of strategy, I'll give them that, but **devastating for how it influenced our culture.**

Although the campaign was meant to help women grow in self-confidence and be more accepting of themselves, the undertones of the campaign were still: *confidence = beauty = skin,* a toxic message that has affected both men and women.

For hundreds and even thousands of years before the campaign, mothers taught their daughters (and sons) the exact opposite, quoting scriptures and sayings such as:

"For the LORD sees not as man sees: man looks on the outward appearance, but the LORD looks on the heart." (1 Samuel 16:7)

"Your beauty should not come from outward adornment, such as elaborate hairstyles and the wearing of gold jewelry or fine clothes. Rather, it should be that of your inner self, the unfading beauty of a gentle and quiet spirit" (1 Peter 3:3-4, NIV)

"No matter how plain a woman may be, if truth and honesty are written across her face, she will be beautiful." — Eleanor Roosevelt

"True beauty, in a Woman, is reflected in her soul. It is the caring that she lovingly gives, the passion that she knows." — Audrey Hepburn

See the difference? While the campaign focused on developing confidence in physical qualities, the focus should really be on the heart (the inner person) —

that's the source of true beauty and confidence.

Today, more than ever before, we are bombarded with messages that convey, *"You are not enough. You are not attractive enough. You are not funny enough. You are not likable enough. You do not have enough. You're not as cool as that guy over there. And you're not as talented as this person over here… But if you try this product, or that, or go to this gym, or do that… you just might be worth something someday. Until then, however, you're destined to be lonely and unlikeable."*

Have you noticed these types of messages? No wonder so many people struggle with depression, self-esteem, and self-worth!

So what is confidence *really*? Where does it come from, and how do you develop it if you're struggling? First, we'll start with what confidence is **not**.

Confidence is not:

- Being attractive
- Being wealthy
- Having nice things
- Having followers, fans, or admirers
- Being successful
- Being talented
- Getting recognition or praise
- Having a relationship or exciting romantic life

But how can you be sure that none of these things will help you feel confident and happy long-term? Simple. Because many of the world's wealthiest, most 'successful', and most 'attractive' people are also the most *insecure*. They commonly struggle with depression and anxiety, get surgery after surgery to change what they can't accept, and many have even committed suicide over their fears of not living up to others' expectations!

Imagine that, seeming to have everything in the world, yet still not being happy with yourself!

The reason for this is that confidence is not *external*. It is ***internal***. Self-confidence and self-esteem can't come from *how others view you,* or *external factors* such as appearance or wealth. **Self**-confidence and **self**-esteem ***must be based on your relationship with yourself.***

A healthy relationship with yourself is one that is kind, supportive, and forgiving. It is one of introspection, contemplation, and healthy hobbies. It involves the healthy self-talk we've covered in other sections and requires the development of healthy habits, self-discipline, and learning to listen to the needs of your body and mind. As you develop a healthy relationship with ***yourself,*** you will feel more confident, more happy, and less alone!

Journaling:

How would you describe your relationship with yourself?

_____

_____

_____

_____

What are your best character qualities?

_____

_____

_____

_____

What personal accomplishments are you proud of?

_____

_____

_____

_____

What have you based your self-esteem or confidence (or lack of it) on until now?

_____

_____

_____

_____

Next, we'll look at the two main virtues, or character qualities, that are the foundation of confidence: integrity and humility.

Integrity

> "Goodness is about character - integrity, honesty, kindness, generosity, moral courage, and the like. More than anything else, it is about how we treat other people." — Dennis Prager

> "Integrity is doing the right thing when you don't have to — when no one else is looking or will ever know — when there will be no congratulations or recognition for having done so." — Charles W. Marshall

According to the American Heritage Dictionary, **integrity** is defined as *"1) Steadfast adherence to a strict moral or ethical code, 2) the state of being unimpaired; soundness, 3) the quality or condition of being whole or undivided;*

completeness."

Integrity is essentially being morally straight in thought, word, and deed, both in the presence of others and when no one is looking. It is being 100% true to your core values and beliefs, and adhering to what you know to be right.

A man of integrity is confident with a deep sense of peace. Because his choices are built on a solid foundation of values, he is not concerned with the judgment of others. He sleeps peacefully knowing he did his best. He is not perfect, as none of us are, but he has a clear determination to improve and keep trying.

Pornography, by contrast, decreases confidence and self-esteem. It is a secret habit that contradicts who you want to be and how you want others to see you. In fact, most men report that they would never do or participate in the things they watch in porn in real life. In one study, 49% of men even report that the content they are watching now is darker than what they used to deem acceptable. This is in part why it causes so many issues with guilt, confidence, and self-worth. *It causes you to act in direct defiance of your natural internal values.*

As Abraham Lincoln once said, quoting a similar Bible passage, *"A house divided cannot stand."* Likewise, self-confidence means being "undivided" or adhering to your moral values with full purpose of heart. It requires self-respect to stick to your goals and do what's best for yourself. As you work towards this, you will feel your confidence improve.

Additionally, having a clean mind and a clear conscience will dramatically improve your self-esteem. A mind full of darkness attracts fear, chaos, hate, and shame, whereas a mind full of virtue attracts peace and joy. Shifting your thoughts from "sex" to personal development and service will help you feel happier and give you greater self-worth than any other pursuit.

As Buckminster Fuller, an influential architect and inventor, put it, *"Integrity is the essence of **everything successful.**"*

Do you feel your choices and habits represent your core values? Why or why not?

_____

_____

_____

_____

Do you feel you are divided or determined in your direction and choices?

_____

_____

_____

_____

As you shift your focus away from sex, masturbation, and porn, what positive things can you transfer your thoughts and focus to?

_____

_____

_____

_____

_____

_____

_____

_____

What positive choices are you making in your life now that you feel good about?

_____

_____

_____

_____

_____

_____

What character qualities are most important to you?

_____

_____

_____

_____

_____

_____

_____

_____

20. HUMILITY & MODESTY

"A superior man is modest in his speech, but exceeds in his actions." — Confucius

"It well becomes a young man to be modest." — Plautus

"A grateful heart is a beginning of greatness. It is an expression of humility. It is a foundation for the development of such virtues as prayer, faith, courage, contentment, happiness, love, and well-being." — James E. Faust

Humility is not thinking less of yourself, it's thinking of yourself less." — Rick Warren

George Washington, the first president of the United States, was an incredible example of humility and modesty. His inaugural procession was described as having all the pomp of a "royal coronation," with 8 days of ceremonies and honorary dinners. Although he was treated like a king, the Father of our nation carried himself very differently. To his Inauguration Ceremony, he wore only a basic, brown broadcloth suit (the cheapest suit that money could buy), making a bold statement.

George Washington was brilliant, wealthy, and had defeated the British army, the largest and most well-disciplined army in the world at the time, and yet he didn't esteem himself above his fellow citizens. He was humble and modest.

Though some associate humility with low self-esteem, I prefer this definition from Webster's 1828 Dictionary stating that humility is: "In ethics, freedom from pride and arrogance; humbleness of mind; a modest estimate of one's own worth."

Rather than low self-esteem, humility is having a modest assessment of your strengths and a realistic acceptance of your weaknesses. It is being honest with yourself and others about where you're at — an honesty that is both freeing and empowering. Instead of the prideful version of "confidence," which over-sells, under-delivers, and denies everything unpleasant, humility is honest and accepting. It seeks growth, but is at peace.

Modesty, on the other hand, goes beyond self-assessment though. Modesty is essentially the intentional practice of not drawing attention to oneself. The 1828 Dictionary defines it as, "not forward or bold; not boastful; not loose or lewd; not excessive or extreme; moderate; decent; in females it is used synonymously with chastity or purity of manners."

George Washington's inaugural wardrobe choice was a beautiful example of this. He had been unanimously voted as the leader of the free world and yet he bowed to those that bowed to him and dressed in the plainest suit money could buy.

True confidence doesn't seek the attention of others because it doesn't need validation. It is kind, modest, and unpresumptuous. Those who seek attention need it. Those who don't are confident enough without it.

As Rudyard Kipling put it in his classic poem 'If':

> *If you can talk with crowds and keep your virtue,*
> *Or walk with Kings — nor lose the common touch...*
> *Yours is the Earth and everything that's in it,*
> *And — which is more — you'll be a Man, my son!*

Journaling:

How might the pursuit of or need for validation hurt one's self-confidence?

_____

_____

_____

_____

How might modesty and humility benefit a person?

Do you tend to like prideful or humble people more? Which is more attractive?

How can you be more humble in your heart and actions?

21. Leaving Your Comfort Zone

"Life begins at the end of your comfort zone." — Neale Donald Walsch

"Acknowledging the unproductive thoughts and ineffective behavior that you've tried to ignore can be uncomfortable. But, stepping out of your comfort zone and choosing to proactively address bad habits will skyrocket your ability to create long-lasting change." — Amy Morin

Judith Bardwick first coined the term "comfort zone" defining it as, "The comfort zone is a behavioral state within which a person operates in an anxiety-neutral condition, using a limited set of behaviors to deliver a steady level of performance, usually without a sense of risk." Essentially, it comes down to the idea that without fear or motivation, most of us don't *move*!

Oftentimes the challenges of life, such as deadlines or a move, will push us out of our comfort zones, but we can also actively seek out experiences that will help us into the growth and learning zones. In these spaces we explore new ideas, act creatively, and push ourselves harder. Joining an addiction recovery program, attending meetings, sharing your story with others, and letting go of old habits and coping mechanisms are all examples! Furthermore, by regularly trying new things, elevating your expectations of yourself, and taking on new challenges, you will experience great personal growth.

Challenge:

Come up with a plan to do something out of your comfort zone this week. Here are a few examples: 1. Do everyday things differently, 2. Mix up your routine, 3. Learn something new, 4. Accept a challenge, 5. Question your beliefs, 6. Practice transparency. What will you do?

_____

_____

_____

22. Loneliness

"Loneliness is the poverty of self; solitude is the richness of self." — May Sarton

"Pray that your loneliness may spur you into finding something to live for, great enough to die for." — Dag Hammarskjold

"Man's loneliness is but his fear of life." — Eugene O'Neill

"Loneliness is and always has been the central and inevitable experience of every man." — Thomas Wolfe

"Loneliness" is unsurprisingly one of the top reported triggers leading to porn, masturbation, and other addictions. Whether you are in a relationship or single, with loving family and friends, or in an isolated location, loneliness seems to be a universal human struggle. In this section, we're going to look at what loneliness is, and if it's *really* the root of the problem. Just how much of the feeling of loneliness is really a lack of connection versus something else?

While most often people think of loneliness as "feeling alone" or lacking family, friends, or a romantic partner, we're going to dig a little deeper.

First, we know it's possible to *feel* alone and not *be* alone. We also know it's possible to *be* alone and not *feel lonely*. So, it seems that the presence of others is not necessarily the cause of *loneliness*. Then what is it?

Whenever we have a void in our life or a need we should ask the question: "Why? Why do I need this? What exactly is the need or the void I am trying to fill?"

Think of an infant child lying alone, un-swaddled. The uncertainty of exposure causes it to kick and cry out for help and comfort. The longer the child is left unattended, the louder it cries out for attention until he or she can hardly breathe.

As an adult, you recognize the child is in no real danger. You might be just a few feet away, yet to the infant that feels lightyears away! He or she cannot comprehend the briefness of its circumstance or your location on the other side of the room. All it knows is the paralyzing fear of being *alone.*

Unfortunately, as adults, we haven't entirely grown out of this fear. Think about it. How do you feel at home alone? Is it uncomfortable? Do you crave attention and emotional comfort? Does loneliness give you anxiety or fear of the future? Do you worry about how long you might be alone? Is it uncomfortable to go out and enjoy experiences alone such as the movies?

Self-validating and self-soothing is a necessary part of maturity. It's the ability to diagnose and process your own emotions and discomfort without the need of others. It is embracing your independence with confidence. That's not to say we don't need or can't enjoy human connection, or that receiving comfort from a friend or loved one is a *bad* thing, but that the ability to go on even without it is critical.

Oftentimes this takes conscious effort. It's the decision to "handle your business" so to speak. It is saying "I can process my own emotions effectively without the need of a pacifier (or porn, for example)!" It comes in stepping out of your comfort zone perhaps to enjoy yourself, to make time for yourself, and to choose, (yes choose!) to be content alone.

One meditation, suggested by Eckhart Tolle, is to think about your problems in this precise moment. What problems do you really have in *this* moment? Is loneliness a problem right now? Or are you okay right now? Is your loneliness a fear of the future? Or are you in dire and immediate need? More likely than not, you are okay at this moment. Focus on that! Remind yourself to remain in the present!

Journaling:

Is your relationship with yourself uncomfortable or enjoyable?

_____

_____

_____

_____

Where does your loneliness come from? What triggers make you feel most alone?

_____

_____

_____

_____

What steps can you take to self-validate, self-soothe, or fix those problems independently?

_____

_____

_____

_____

How might *neediness* interfere with finding or developing a healthy relationship with the right person?

_____

_____

_____

In what ways have you neglected your relationship with yourself?

What activities or experiences can you plan to do with yourself that you will enjoy?

Affirmations:

- I'm doing great!
- I can have a fulfilling relationship with myself.
- I can enjoy this moment with myself.
- I choose to be whole.

23. DISCOVERING YOUR VALUES

"If you can quit for a day, you can quit for a lifetime." — Benjamin Alire Sáenz

"Oh man! Live your own life and you will no longer be wretched. Keep to your appointed place in the order of nature and nothing can tear you from it." — Jean-Jacques Rousseau

The most important and powerful question I've ever been asked was, "*What do you crave most?*"

I had been suffering from extreme anxiety and depression for about three months. I would wake up every morning in a panic attack. I couldn't eat and the fatigue was crushing my productivity. It was time to do something about it, and my family was pressuring me to see a doctor.

Then one day, a friend of mine who's also a life coach asked me the question, "What do you crave most?"

I thought about it and immediately a memory came to mind. "THAT. That is what I crave most," I thought. But what was it specifically about that experience, I wondered. So, I locked myself in my room to meditate and journal. I came up with a list of several things that I needed and wanted more of: connection, food, experience, peace, and acceptance. Then I pondered on the question, "What do I need to do to have those things?" The second I came up with the answer was the end of my anxiety and depression. Isn't that amazing!? *All* my symptoms were gone the next day. I then created a new life plan in line with my values, and things started to look up again.

When a person is living in line with his or her core values, they have energy, motivation, passion, focus, and deep peace of mind. Living your core values also puts you more in line with your *natural role,* which is the only place you can be truly happy. Your goal today is to identify and define your own core values and the changes you need to make to live them more fully.

Journaling:

Who is someone you deeply admire?

_____

_____

What is it about them that inspires you?

_____

_____

_____

_____

What admirable qualities do they possess?

_____

_____

_____

_____

Which of their behaviors and actions would you like to emulate?

_____

_____

_____

_____

What else inspires or motivates you?

_____

_____

_____

_____

What causes are you passionate about?

_____

_____

_____

_____

What things are you willing to passionately defend? (People, values, principles, things, etc.)

_____

_____

_____

_____

When you act in a positive way that's in harmony with your core values, what do you gain? What feelings do you have?

_____

_____

When do you feel most like yourself?

What situations make you feel uncomfortable and why?

In what situations do you feel real and authentic?

What positive emotions or outcomes do you experience?

_____

_____

_____

_____

What do you crave most in life right now?

_____

_____

_____

_____

What are the deepest wishes of your heart?

_____

_____

_____

_____

What does a perfect day look like for you?

_____

_____

_____

_____

_____

_____

Where do you feel most at peace?

_____

_____

_____

_____

What values do those things or places represent?

_____

_____

_____

_____

What qualities do they have, or what needs do they satisfy?

_____

_____

_____

_____

VALUES LIST

Identify the core values you most resonate with by placing a line through those you are unconcerned with, and circling those that stand out to you.

- Adventure
- Altruism
- Authenticity
- Balance
- Beauty
- Career
- Charisma
- Communication
- Compassion
- Competition
- Connection
- Cooperation
- Courage
- Creativity
- Duty
- Effectiveness
- Encouragement
- Excellence
- Excitement
- Experience
- Fame
- Family
- Fitness
- Forgiveness
- Freedom
- Friendship
- Fun
- Generosity
- "Giving People a Chance"
- Goodness
- Grace
- Gratitude
- Growth
- Happiness
- Harmony
- Health
- Honesty
- Humor
- Innovation
- Integrity
- Intelligence
- Intuition
- Justice
- Kindness
- Leadership
- Learning
- Love
- Loyalty
- Nurturing
- Openness
- Organization
- Patience
- Peace
- Personal Development
- Power
- Professionalism
- Prosperity
- Reciprocity
- Rehabilitation/ Restoration Relationships
- Religion
- Respect
- Security
- Service
- Spirituality
- Strength
- Success
- Teaching
- Teamwork
- Wealth
- Wellness
- Wisdom
- Work

Journaling:

Next, we'll look at how to use what you've learned to create a more meaningful and powerful life. What 3 core values do you believe are most important to you?

_____

_____

_____

_____

What are *you* missing most?

_____

_____

_____

_____

What lifestyle changes can you make to live your values more consistently?

_____

_____

_____

_____

24. What Sex Is, Isn't & Should Be

For this section, I will be using the word the word "sex" to describe any sexual activity or arousal of sexual feelings, whether alone or with another person. This includes masturbation, pornography, sexting, books with sexual themes, fantasizing, dry sex, oral sex, intercourse, the use of sex toys, and any physical touching of the sex organs.

For thousands of years, the topic of sex has captivated the human mind as the subject of art, literature, and philosophy. Fundamentally, sex is an act of procreation — a biological vehicle which produces offspring, but it's so much more, isn't it?

Sex has a powerful effect on the mind. It has the ability to relieve stress, anxiety, and pain. It can clear the head, heal the heart, and create an intense bond with those we share it. It can be a beautiful dance of love and affection and a physical experience of profound pleasure. There is also a spiritual element and many health benefits to sexual activity.

That's how sex is meant to be, but as with many things in life that are fundamentally good, sex can also be misused and become destructive. At the wrong time, in the wrong place, or with the wrong person, sexual experiences can lead to lifelong trauma. Rape, molestation, addiction, and other forms of sexual abuse and misconduct destroy the heart and soul and shake a person to their core.

Our media today is saturated with promiscuity, sexual violence, and sexual comedy which degrades the ideal and beautiful nature of what sexuality can and should be. The biggest problem with this false advertising is the effect on youth, who really don't know any better. With so many mixed messages swirling around about sex and "choice," it's understandably confusing for many people.

Whatever your personal beliefs, I encourage you to challenge them with the following questions: Has the increased sexual permissiveness and hypersexuality in society today had positive or negative effect in your life? And does it lead to happier individuals and families?

Think about it for a moment.

Chances are that you've seen first-hand the negative effects of sexual addiction, sexual abuse, or infidelity in your life, or in the life of someone you love.

While many still deny the deeper spiritual and emotional dimensions of sex, the conversation almost always changes regarding sexual abuse. For example, most people agree that rape is far more serious than battery and that molesting a child is NOT consensual *physical pleasure*. Most governments still enforce strict laws regarding sexual activity with a minor, and most parents still try to protect the innocence of their children.

This brings me to the conclusion that at least part of our society still recognizes this deeper meaning beyond pleasure. Religion teaches there is even something *sacred* to it. Whereas science might point out the powerful hormones that unquestionably lead to bonding.

Whatever your personal beliefs, the highly powerful nature of sex means that both consent and selectiveness are critical factors behind who we share sexual experiences with. I encourage you to spend some time thinking about this.

What messages regarding sexuality have influenced your life positively or negative?

An Act of Love

If you've read anything about healthy eating, you've probably heard that fruit juice isn't healthy, but fruit is. So, what's the difference between an apple and apple juice, you might ask? The difference, aside from chemical processing, is the *fiber*, and the process of digestion. Juice is a concentrated sugar, but fruit is digested and processed in the body much more slowly, allowing the nutrients to be better absorbed.

The relationship between sex and love is similar. Ideally, healthy sexual relationships include the following components: consent, affection, respect, safety, acceptance, commitment (through marriage and lifelong commitment), and real love. However, when any one component is missing, the experience is reduced to simply empty gratification, a 'sugar rush,' an illusion of what we truly desire, and a toxic habit that can destroy us at our core.

Dr. Victor L. Brown, Jr., describes sexual fragmentation this way:

> *"If we relate to each other in fragments, at best we miss full relationships. At worst, we manipulate and exploit others for our gratification.... Sexual fragmentation is particularly harmful because it is particularly deceptive. The intense human intimacy that should be enjoyed in and symbolized by sexual union is counterfeited by sensual episodes which suggest — but cannot deliver — acceptance, understanding, and love. Such encounters mistake the end for the means as lonely, desperate people seek a common denominator which will permit the easiest, quickest gratification."* [Victor L. Brown, Jr., Human Intimacy: Illusion and Reality]

When I work with couples or married men, I am frequently asked, "Should I still have sex with my wife?"

My answer is always this: "Only have sex as an act of love, and not to simply satisfy a biological urge." This way you will be able to enjoy the full experience, create bonding, and cultivate deep intimacy.

If it is truly an act of love:

- You will not be mad if your partner fails to satisfy you or engage in sexual activities at the time or in the way you want.
- You will not feel inclined to turn to porn or masturbation.
- You will not have expectations of performance.
- You will not expect validation from them on your performance.
- You will not value your own wishes over their comfort.

Journaling:

If you are single, spend some time meditating on and recording your thoughts on your ideal loving, relationship and partnership. Make a note of sexual thoughts that have polluted your mind or distracted you from this goal.

If you are married or in a relationship, write down a few ways you can better love and serve your partner to cultivate deeper intimacy.

_____

_____

_____

_____

_____

_____

_____

_____

_____

_____

_____

_____

_____

_____

_____

25. MAKING AMENDS

"Not admitting a mistake is a bigger mistake." — Robert Half

"Sincere apologies are for those that make them, not for those to whom they are made." — Greg LeMond

"Never ruin an apology with an excuse." — Benjamin Franklin

There comes a time in your journey of growth and healing where you will feel remorse for the things you've done, and the desire to make amends to those you have hurt. It's been said that the best apology is changed behavior, and while that's very true, there is also healing in the admission of your wrong doings.

It takes a lot of strength and courage to admit when you're wrong and to apologize for the things you've done. There is a lot of strength and healing in it though. It will help you to move forward from guilt and shame, and as a result, you'll feel greater strength and confidence in yourself. Regardless of the outcome or whether the other person chooses to forgive, you can find peace, knowing you did what's right to make amends.

8 Elements of a Proper Apology:

1. **Sincerity.** Before even thinking about approaching another person to make amends, make sure your apology is coming from a place of sincere regret and humility. If your apology is not sincere, the other person will feel it.

2. **Acknowledge responsibility.** Take ownership, and admit your mistakes. Even if mistakes were made by both parties, focus only on your actions in your apology.

3. **Expression of regret.** This is the part where you say, "I'm sorry" and express genuine remorse for your actions. Consider reading the book, *"The 5 Languages of Apology"* by Gary Chapman, as he highlights the

different preferences people have, when it comes to apologizing. It's a very helpful resource.

4. **Acknowledgment of what went wrong**. Demonstrate that you understand where you went wrong, and that you have learned from it. It's important to not make excuses though.

5. **Declaration of repentance**. This is an opportunity to let the person know you intend to change, and that you won't let the mistake happen again.

6. **Offer of repair**. Where possible, offer to make up for the damage you caused.

7. **Request for forgiveness**. Depending on the emotional connection between you and the person you've wronged, you may want to ask for forgiveness. This gives you and the other person an opportunity to repair the relationship. Even if that request is denied, at least you will have peace knowing you did your best.

8. **Change**. This is the most important step. Establish a plan to make sure the mistake doesn't happen again, and commit to making progress in correcting or improving your conduct. Most importantly, prove your apology is sincere, by *demonstrating* your change moving forward.

Activity:

Make a plan according to the eight elements above to make amends for something you've done in the past that you now regret. Write your plan below.

_____

_____

_____

_____

How do you feel after completing the above task?

Affirmations:

- Forgiveness is a gift I can give myself.
- I am proud of myself for doing what's right.
- I can learn and grow from my mistake.

26. THE PURPOSE OF DOUBT

"Be miserable. Or motivate yourself. Whatever must be done, it's always your choice." — Wayne Dyer

"Doubt must be no more than vigilance, otherwise it can become dangerous." — Georg C. Lichtenberg

"I have self-doubt. I have insecurity. I have a fear of failure. I have nights when I show up at the arena and I'm like, 'My back hurts, my feet hurt, my knees hurt. I don't have it. I just want to chill.' We all have self-doubt. You don't deny it, but you also don't capitulate to it. You embrace it." — Kobe Bryant

"Modest doubt is called the beacon of the wise." — William Shakespeare

My initial plan for this lesson was peppy and motivational — some sort of trendy "You're amazing. Don't doubt yourself" type message.

As I was searching for quotes, however, I found that only modern "influencers" used the expression "don't doubt yourself," yet practically all the ancient philosophers *embraced* doubt, and even *promoted* it! That was surprising to me, so I spent some time analyzing their opinions and explanations.

I invite you today to carefully consider and meditate on the following quotes:

"Doubt is the beginning of wisdom." — Aristotle

"Doubt is not a pleasant condition, but certainty is absurd." — Voltaire

"There lives more faith in honest doubt, believe me, than in half the creeds." — Alfred Lord Tennyson

Below are a few additional examples to consider of how your doubts may actually *benefit* you:

- Doubt helps us identify areas of weakness and potential problems.
- It keeps us balanced and grounded.
- It tests your commitment and causes you to think deeply about your purpose and intentions.
- It provides feedback. Like any good coach, our doubts provide important feedback that can help us reach our goals. Without that, we wouldn't be able to improve.

Journaling:

What do your doubts *provide you*? Why is it a good thing, and how can you embrace it in a healthy way?

_____

_____

_____

_____

_____

Now, consider these 4 ways to embrace, utilize, and work *with* doubts:

#1. Filter:

- Are your doubts productive/constructive, or demotivating/toxic?
- Do they follow the THINK model? (Is the thought: true, helpful, inspiring, necessary, and kind?)
- Are the doubts holding you back or warning you about something?
- Are they valid concerns?

#2. Analyze:

- What areas of weakness do your doubts highlight?
- What can you take ownership of to prevent failure?
- What can you do differently to secure success?

#3. Rewrite:

- What can you say differently to yourself (Using the THINK model)?

#4. Push forward

If your goal is important and worthwhile, and you have addressed potential problems or weaknesses, it's time to push forward anyway! Adopt some supportive phrases like *"I'll do my best", "It's worth a shot"*, and even *"I can do this"* that will help you push through the negative thoughts. When it comes to recovery, your **motivating reason** should inspire you to keep fighting to overcome any doubts and obstacles along the way.

Journaling:

Share your analysis of one restricting/toxic doubt, and how you can use it and rewrite it for your success?

_____

_____

_____

_____

_____

_____

_____

27. Habits & Muscle Memory

"There is no influence like the influence of habit." — Gilbert Parker

"Laziness is nothing more than the habit of resting before you get tired." — Jules Renard

Have you ever deleted a popular social media app, and then later tried to open it anyway? This kind of unconscious, automatic behavior can have a heavy influence on addiction and the recovery process. A compulsive habit such as constantly checking your phone can even be classified as an addiction! Studies have found that most relapses happen at a regular time and place. This means that most people relapse the same way. Part of the reason for this may be convenience or triggers, but a lot of it has to do with habit and muscle memory.

Just as walking into a restroom can give you the urge to use the toilet, even if you didn't need to before, opening your phone late at night or being alone in your bedroom can cause a similar habitual reaction to view porn. To cope with these reactions, it's important to develop new habits that counteract them. For instance, you could consider developing a new bedtime routine or training yourself to pick up a book instead of your phone when you're bored.

By replacing your old routines with something new, you will slowly weaken and override your old habit associations and triggers.

Activity:

Choose one small habit to conquer/change this week. Aim for seven consecutive days: ☐ ☐ ☐ ☐ ☐ ☐ ☐

28. Gratitude

"When you are grateful, fear disappears, and abundance appears." — Tony Robbins

"Gratitude is the ability to experience life as a gift. It liberates us from the prison of self — preoccupation." — John Ortberg

"If you concentrate on finding whatever is good in every situation, you will discover that your life will suddenly be filled with gratitude, a feeling that nurtures the soul." — Harold Kushner

Gratitude is a beautiful, but often forgotten part of recovery. Though you may have begun this journey on principle alone, gratitude is the fuel which will carry you through to lifelong success. As you acknowledge your progress in recovery and experience the ongoing benefits of staying clean, your confidence and motivation will increase, and your fears and regrets will decrease.

Through sincere gratitude, your relationship with yourself and God will also heal and strengthen.

Journaling:

Gratitude in all aspects of our lives helps us to be happier, and when it comes to recovery, it brings a special power and strength to the process.

What benefits have you experienced so far in this journey?

_____

_____

_____

_____

How have you grown as a person since you started your recovery?

___

What physical benefits have you noticed?

___

How have your relationships improved?

How have your friends, family, God, or others helped you along the way?

What other aspects of this process are you grateful for?

29. Natural Law

"Every person has free choice. Free to obey or disobey the Natural Laws. Your choice determines the consequences." — Alfred A. Montapert

"The Tao, which others may call Natural Law or Traditional Morality or the First Principles of Practical Reason or the First Platitudes, is not one among a series of possible systems of value. It is the sole source of all value judgments. If it is rejected, all value is rejected. If any value is retained, it is retained." — C.S. Lewis

"You may hate gravity, but gravity doesn't care." — Clayton M. Christensen

Natural law and the laws of human nature are as real as gravity. For example, if you throw something into the air, it always comes down. It may get briefly stuck in a tree, but it will always come down *eventually*. This is natural law. Put another way, all actions have consequences.

Obedience to natural laws is for our own benefit, whereas rejecting those laws often leads to weakness and unhappiness. This is inescapable. Although we may attempt to run from natural laws and pretend like they don't exist, the consequences and outcomes will always catch up with us.

Let's expand on this, with a specific example of trust. When we are dishonest, we lose the trust and respect of those around us. Sometimes, without even knowing the truth, people will treat us differently simply because they "sense something suspicious." The natural law at work here is that dishonesty creates distrust, and distrust is not good for relationships. Therefore, by extension, *dishonesty is not good for society,* because society is made up of *relationships* and relationships are damaged by dishonesty.

Although increasingly unpopular in the 'mainstream', the laws of ancient morality have been proven over thousands of years to produce positive outcomes for both individuals and society. This objective is what we will call the 'highest good' — or the pursuit of the most favorable outcomes for the greatest number of people.

Pursuing the *highest good* in your life means making those choices, often difficult to master, that secure a permeating and lasting joy for yourself and those you love. In other words: **doing what's right.** This is the core of religion, and the foundation of a healthy society.

Journaling:

Try to identify a natural law and the positive and negative consequences associated with them. First, think of an unhealthy or "immoral" practice or behavior. What is it?

_____

_____

_____

_____

Who is negatively affected by this practice or behavior?

_____

_____

_____

What predictable consequences are associated?

_____

_____

_____

What is the natural law at work here?

Why is it important for individuals, families, and societies to honor this natural law?

What are the benefits of observance?

Affirmations:

- I am in control of who I become.
- I have a purpose and a role to play

30. Pride vs. Healthy Self-Esteem

"A man's pride can be his downfall, and he needs to learn when to turn to others for support and guidance." — Bear Grylls

"Confidence turns into pride only when you are in denial of your mistakes." — Criss Jami

Pride, a close cousin to ego, has many negative effects on our lives. Though the word pride is often used as a good thing (e.g., cultural pride, pride in your work) there is an important distinction to make between *healthy* pride and the kind of pride that's destructive.

Ezra Taft Benson, Former Secretary of Agriculture for the United States and a prominent religious leader said, *"Most of us think of pride as self-centeredness, conceit, boastfulness, arrogance, or haughtiness. All of these are elements... but the heart, or core, is still missing. The central feature of pride is enmity — enmity toward God and enmity toward our fellowmen. Enmity means 'hatred toward, hostility to, or a state of opposition.'"*

Consider These Comparisons:

<u>Pride:</u> Compares, judges, feels defensive, resists change, resists wisdom, doesn't listen to help, doesn't want help, feels everything is fine.

<u>Healthy Confidence:</u> Accepts faults, acknowledges weaknesses, acknowledges strengths, is full of gratitude

It's been said that the opposite of pride is not humility but rather *love*. Because pride stems from enmity or hate, the solution involves developing real love for yourself, for God, and others.

Humility comes from accepting our natural role as a part of the universe rather than in opposition to it. It comes from finding peace and harmony with God and mankind, and not ranking ourselves any higher or lower, or better or worse, than any other.

One thing is certain about pride though: life will always find a way to humble us if we don't!

Here are a few simple ways to develop humility:

- Be grateful
- Be honest
- Accept shortcomings & mistakes with a desire to be better
- Don't worry what others think
- Accept reality, and be patient with the "flow" and circumstances of life
- Serve others generously, lovingly, and selflessly

Another tool for overcoming pride is *acceptance (a quality of love)*.

Think of the world as a mirror. What you see reflects what's inside of YOU, and what you hate most in others is almost always a reflection of something that exists in you. What you hate in yourself, you hate in others. What you accept in yourself, you can accept in the world around you.

The following activity will help you to not only be more humble, but also to be more patient, accepting, and loving with others.

Activity:

Begin by writing a list of frustrations you have towards a specific person (perhaps a relative, partner, child, co-worker, or an ex):

_____

_____

_____

_____

Next, for every item on that list, work to identify at least one way YOU demonstrate that same behavior or a related attribute. For example, could it be that frustration towards an impatient coworker reflects your own impatience at home? Frustration towards a partner for running late may reflect your own issues with procrastination.

Continue working on your list until you have identified your own reflection for each of the above frustrations. If necessary, you might ask a partner or friend for their help to identify examples, and if you do that, be willing to listen carefully without judgment!

_____

_____

_____

_____

Now, without judging yourself, take ownership. Accept those behaviors and attributes fully in yourself. For each, write down at least one positive outcome or benefit of the attribute or behavior.

_____

_____

_____

_____

_____

How does it make you feel to see these attributes in yourself?

_____

_____

_____

_____

_____

How can you be more forgiving and patient when you see these attributes or behaviors in others?

_____

_____

_____

_____

_____

Affirmations:

- I accept myself.
- I love myself.
- I allow myself to grow and change.

DAY 30 CLEAN: DO YOU WANT TO CONTINUE?

"Press forward. Do not stop, do not linger in your journey, but strive for the mark set before you." — George Whitefield

Congratulations! You've completed each of the principles and strategies for recovery. It's time for the big question: *Do you want to continue making progress?*

Thirty days is a key benchmark in the recovery process and a good place to assess the benefits and drawbacks. If you haven't reached a full 30 days of sobriety yet, I highly recommend pushing yourself to achieve that goal before making any decisions.

Hopefully this has been an inspiring and helpful journey for you! Ponder on and answer the following questions as a part of your assessment.

On a personal note, I want to thank you for the work and time you have put into your recovery. This is such an important cause and I am honored that you allowed *Fight The Beast* and myself to be a part of your journey!

Whether you are currently at 5 days, 30 days, or 365+ in your recovery, I hope you make the choice to press on, stay focused, and continue striving for your goals. **To be among the 2% who are consistently porn free is a huge accomplishment, and you deserve sincere commendation.** By your courageous actions and self-discipline, you will bless the lives of all those around you.

You are unique, powerful, and special. You have *so* much to offer the world, and the fact that you've studied this book represents a powerful step in your journey.

As I've said many times before, connecting with *Fight The Beast* online will ***greatly improve your likelihood of long-term freedom from sexual addiction.***

Please visit: **www.FightTheBeast.org** today, and I look forward to welcoming you to our wonderful community of like-minded men and women who are committed to their recovery.

Journaling:

How do you feel overall about your journey so far?

_____

_____

_____

_____

_____

_____

_____

_____

_____

_____

_____

_____

_____

_____

_____

What successful changes have you made?

What benefits have you seen or felt?

How has your life improved?

What additional changes would you like to achieve or what additional benefits would you like to see?

What steps can you take to get more out of this journey and achieve your goals?

What challenges have you encountered?

What steps could you take to work through or alleviate these challenges?

What are the benefits of pressing forward?

Do you want to continue this lifestyle of freedom from porn and/or sexual addiction?

Additional thoughts:

Additional Daily Review Page

DAILY REVIEW

Streak Length: _____   **Days to Goal:** _____   **Did you succeed today?** _____

1. How would you rate your urges on a scale of 0-10? *(Give yourself a pat on the back if they were higher than normal and you still succeeded!)* _____

2. How would you rate your mood on a scale of 0-10? _____

3. How would you rate your energy on a scale of 0-10? _____

4. What else did you succeed in today?

   _____

   _____

5. What can you do better tomorrow?

   _____

   _____

6. What is something for which you are grateful today?

   _____

   _____

7. Progress Notes:

   _____

   _____

   _____

Made in the USA
Columbia, SC
15 January 2024